Norwegian Cookbook

Traditional Scandinavian Recipes Made Easy

Introduction

I would like to thank and congratulate you for buying this book, *'Norwegian Cookbook: Traditional Scandinavian Recipes Made Easy'* and hope that you find this book interesting, helpful and informative in your bid to learn about Norwegian cuisine.

It is almost impossible to find a person in this world who does not love food. It is one of those pleasures that everyone loves to indulge in, especially since there is such a wide variety of cuisine and meal styles around the world. The food habits of people and cultures are so varied that it is possible to find 3-4 different types of cuisine in the radius of 10 square miles. This is because we, as humans, love food and secondly we have learned to adapt to our surroundings.

Despite the vast culture and food choices across the world, almost everyone has started eating pretty much the same things thanks to capitalism and the ever-rising fast food industry. However, not only are these foods bad for your body, but they are often tasteless as compared to traditional and recipes that are culturally deep rooted. Many people want to cook traditional recipes. However, they think it is tedious and elaborate, and thus give in to the fast food industry. But the fact of the matter here is not learning your traditional recipes is akin to slowly killing your culture and its rich legacy.

To keep in touch with your cultural roots or those of the other rich heritages around the world, this is the perfect book for you. This book will help you cook the traditional recipes of the beautiful Scandinavian nation of Norway.

Norwegian cuisine is a highly varied cuisine with different dishes and recipes that can only be found in Norway and other Scandinavian regions. A cuisine that is heavy on stored items and game meats, everyone can find something to eat that they will enjoy. Blessed with beautiful wildlife as well as one of the longest coastlines in the world, Norwegian cuisine is full of meat and fish dishes. Norwegian cod and salmon are famous throughout the world. Norway is also famous for its lamb as most of the animals are fed naturally, making their meat tender and extremely juicy.

Since people will try these recipes across the world, we have restricted the use of game meat and used readily available fish and meats. The ingredients are also quite simple and will be available in almost every farmers' market.

So without any further delay, let us get started!

Thanks again for purchasing this book. I hope you enjoy it!

Table of Content

Chapter One: Norwegian Breakfast Recipes................................ 1

Norwegian Thin Pancakes...1

Baked Cheese Omelet...3

Risengryn - Norwegian Rice Porridge.................................4

Blueberry Breakfast Crepes...5

Real Swedish Pancakes 7

Swedish Scrambled Eggs..8

Danish Kringle 9

Ableskiver – Danish Doughnuts 10

Rugbrod - Scandinavian Rye Bread 11

Danish Bubble...13

Open face Salmon and Egg Scandinavian Sandwich 15

Hazelnut Butter & Strawberry Sandwich.........................16

Raisin Scones..17

Biksemad - Scandinavian Hash..19

Danish Rolls 20

Norwegian Romme Grot...22

Creamy Curried Egg Salad Sandwich...............................23

Scandinavian Breakfast Muesli 24

Ollebrod - Danish Rye Bread Porridge.............................25

Chapter Two: Norwegian Lunch Recipes..........................27

Skagen Toast..27

Herring Sandwiches..28

Gravlax Club Sandwich...29

Scandinavian Chicken...31

Norwegian Fish Cakes with Dill Mayonnaise..................33

Danish Glazed Mushrooms..35

Potato Pancakes...36

Blue Cheese, Pear, and Hazelnut Smørrebrød................37

Shrimp Egg and Dill Smorrebrod...................................38

Venison Sandwich with Bacon, Chestnut Crème Fraiche and
Lingonberry jam...39

Lindström Patties...41

Chapter Three: Norwegian Dinner Recipes...............**43**

Sautéed Chicken with Caraway and Cream....................43

Scandinavian Chicken and Cabbage..............................45

Chicken with Rosemary and Juniper.............................47

Norwegian Chicken Braised with Dried Fruit.................48

Fried Herring Pickled in Liquor....................................50

Pike Perch with Creamed Mushrooms and Horseradish Butter...........52

Pasta with Crayfish..54

Roast Pork Loin with Salted Caramel Potatoes..............56

Wiener schnitzel..59

Scandinavian Meatballs with Mash and Lingonberry Sauce...................61

Swedish Meat Pies 63

Biff stroganoff - Beef stroganoff 65

Lammstek med Timjan-rödvinsås -Roast Lamb with Thyme and Red Wine Sauce 67

Creamed Spinach with Crumbled Egg Yolks 69

Scandinavian Mashed Potato and Rutabaga Casserole 71

Vegetables Au Gratin 73

Vegan Kjottkaker – Lentil Cakes with Gravy 74

Onion Pie with Jarlsberg and Thyme 76

Scandinavian Noodles 78

Pumpkin Soup with Orange and Parmigiano Reggiano 79

Celery Root, Carrot and Potato Gratin 81

Cod with Potatoes and Sundried Tomato Pesto 83

Swedish Turkey Meatballs 85

Pork Chops 87

Fårikål - Norwegian Lamb & Cabbage Stew 88

Smordampete nypoteter - Butter Steamed New Potatoes 89

Danish Stegt Flæsk med Persillesovs 90

Swedish Caviar Cake 92

Gravadlax in Dill 94

Kryddad Raudkal Med Blaberjum - Spiced Cabbage with Blueberries 95

Danish Spinach with Pasta 96

Rødkålssalat Med Appelsin 97

Lammekolle pa Gronsager 98

Skinkefars med broccolifyld 99

Pan Seared White Fish with Mussels, Cabbage Shoots and Cream.....101

Chapter Four: Norwegian Soup Recipes.................. 104

Knefla Soup 104

Creamy Spinach Soup with Dill 106

Hvidløgssuppe..108

Scandinavian Cabbage Soup 110

Squashsuppe..112

Grøn Løgsuppe...113

Juliennesuppe...115

Scandinavian Vegetable Soup with Shrimp 116

Scandinavian Chicken Soup 118

Kjotsupa - Lamb Soup 120

Scandinavian Raspberry Soup..................................122

Kold Sommersuppe 124

Chapter Five: Norwegian Salad Recipes................... 126

Celery and Blue Cheese Salad 126

Danish Potato Salad 127

Danish Cucumber Salad 129

Scandinavian Cucumber Salad.................................130

Smoked Salmon Salad 131

Blue Cheese, Grape and Gem Lettuce Salad...................................... 133

Chapter Six: Norwegian Dessert Recipes.....................135

Swedish Apple Pie... 135

Norwegian Rhubarb Pudding 137

Traditional Swedish Almond Cake.. 138

Norwegian Cookies 140

Swedish Brownies 141

Tilsorte Bondepiker - Veiled Peasant Girls............................. 142

Ostkak - Swedish Cheesecake.. 143

Norwegian Apple Cake... 144

Bringebaerpudding med Bringebaersaus - Raspberry Pudding with Raspberries Sauce.. 145

Strawberry Snow 147

Norwegian Fruit Cake.. 148

Almond Sugar Cookies... 150

Ostkaka med Farska Jordgubbar Och Mynta – Almond Cheesecake with Macerated Strawberries and Mint 152

Drommekage – Danish Dream Cake... 154

Kladdkaka – Swedish "Gooey" Chocolate Cake...................... 156

Honey and Butter Baked Pears with Cold Cream.................... 158

Chapter One: Norwegian Breakfast Recipes

Norwegian Thin Pancakes

Makes: 4 pancakes

Ingredients:

- 1 egg

- 1 ½ cups milk

- 10 tablespoons white flour

- 1 teaspoon granulated sugar

- 1/8 teaspoon salt

- Butter, to grease

Method:

1. Add sugar and egg into a bowl and beat well.

2. Add the milk and salt.

3. Add flour and mix until well combined.

4. Place a skillet over medium heat. Grease with butter.

5. Pour about 2-3 tablespoons of the mixture into the pan. Swirl the pan so that the batter spreads.

6. Cook until golden brown on both sides

7. Repeat the above 3 steps to make the remaining pancakes.

Baked Cheese Omelet

Serves: 2

Ingredients:

- 2 eggs

- ¼ teaspoon salt

- 2 green onions, thinly sliced

- 1 medium bell pepper, deseeded, chopped

- 2 tablespoons water

- 1 tablespoon butter

- ½ cup cooked ham, diced

- 6 ounces Jarlsberg cheese or any other cheese of your choice, cut into ½ inch cubes

- A handful parsley, chopped, to garnish

Method:

1. Add eggs, water and salt into a bowl and whisk well.

2. Place an ovenproof pan over medium heat. Add butter. When butter melts, add onion, bell pepper and ham. Cook for 2-3 minutes. Turn off the heat.

3. Pour egg into the pan. Place cheese cubes on top.

4. Place the pan in a preheated oven.

5. Bake at 400°F for 15-20 minutes or until the omelet is cooked.

6. Garnish with parsley and serve.

3

Risengryn - Norwegian Rice Porridge
Serves: 3

Ingredients:

- 6 tablespoons short grain rice, rinsed, soaked in water for an hour

- ¾ cup water

- 2 cups milk

- ½ teaspoon ground nutmeg

- ¼ cup raisins or black current (optional)

- ½ teaspoon salt

- ½ teaspoon vanilla extract (optional)

To serve: Use as much as required

- Butter

- Sugar

- Milk

- Ground cinnamon

Method:

1. Place a saucepan over medium heat. Add water and bring to the boil.

2. Add rice and stir. Stir in the milk, vanilla and raisins if using. Bring to the boil.

3. Lower heat and cover with a lid. Simmer until rice is tender.

4. Add salt and stir.

5. Ladle into bowls and top with butter, sugar, milk and cinnamon

Blueberry Breakfast Crepes

Serves: 8

Ingredients:

- 6 eggs
- 3 tablespoons butter, melted
- 2 tablespoons sugar
- 6 tablespoons butter or more if required
- Granulated sugar, as required
- Lemon wedges to serve
- 2 cups milk
- 1 ½ cups flour
- ½ teaspoon salt
- 3 cups fresh blueberries
- Powdered sugar, to taste, sifted
- Butter, melted, as required (optional), to serve

Method:

1. Add eggs to a bowl. Whisk well. Add about a tablespoon butter and milk and whisk well.

2. Mix together in a bowl, blueberries and sugar. Set aside.

3. Mix together in a bowl, sugar, flour and salt.

4. Add into the bowl of eggs and whisk well.

5. Place a shallow frying pan of about 8 inches diameter, over medium heat. Add a little of the butter (about ½ tablespoon).

6. When butter melts, spoon about 3 tablespoons of the batter on the pan. Swirl the pan so that the batter spreads.

7. Cook until both sides are golden brown.

8. Place a little of the blueberries on one half of the crepe. Fold the other half over the filling. Carefully slide the crepe on to a plate.

9. Repeat the above 4 steps with the remaining batter to make 7 more crepes.

Real Swedish Pancakes

Serves: 2

Ingredients:

- 1 egg

- 1 ¼ cups milk

- Butter, to fry, as required

- 10 tablespoons plain wheat flour

- ½ teaspoon salt

Method:

1. Add egg flour and salt into a bowl and stir.

2. Pour milk, a little at a time, and mix well each time. You will be left with a very thin batter.

3. Place a skillet over medium heat. Grease with butter.

4. Pour about 2-3 tablespoons of the batter on the pan. Swirl the pan so that the batter spreads.

5. Cook until both sides are golden brown.

6. Carefully slide on to a plate.

7. Repeat the above 3 steps to make the remaining pancakes.

8. You can stack the pancakes after it is cooked. Keep warm until use.

9. Serve with whipped cream and jam of your choice.

Swedish Scrambled Eggs

Serves: 4

Ingredients:

- 8 eggs

- 2 tablespoons fresh dill, finely chopped or 3 teaspoons dried dill

- Salt to taste

- Pepper to taste

- 8 ounces cream cheese, chopped into small cubes

- ¼ teaspoon garlic powder

- Nonstick cooking spray

Method:

1. Add eggs into a bowl and whisk until pale and foamy.

2. Add rest of the ingredients and stir until well combined.

3. Place a skillet over high heat. Spray cooking spray over it.

4. Add the egg mixture into the pan. Lower heat to medium and stir. Scramble and cook the eggs until the consistency you desire is achieved.

Danish Kringle

Makes: 16

Ingredients:

- 2 refrigerated pie crusts, softened as per the instructions on the package

- 2/3 cup packed brown sugar

- 1 cup powdered sugar

- 4-6 teaspoons milk

- 1 1/3 cups pecans, chopped + extra to top

- 6 tablespoons butter, softened

- ½ teaspoon vanilla extract

- Water, as required

Method:

1. Place the piecrusts on a baking sheet. Do not grease the baking sheet.

2. Add pecans, butter and brown sugar in a bowl.

3. Divide the pecan mixture among both the piecrusts and spread on half the crusts. Leave a gap of ¾ inch on the edges. Brush the edges of the piecrust with water.

4. Fold the other half over the filling. Press the edges to seal. Prick the edges as well as the top with a fork.

5. Place the kringles towards the center of the baking sheet.

6. Bake in a preheated oven at 375 °F for 15-20 minutes or until golden brown on top.

7. Cool and slice into wedges and serve.

Ableskiver – Danish Doughnuts

Serves: 5-6

Ingredients:

- 2 cups flour

- 3 teaspoons baking powder

- 4 eggs

- 2 tablespoons sugar

- A pinch salt

- 3 cups milk

Method:

1. Add flour, baking powder, sugar and salt into a bowl and stir.

2. Whisk together eggs and milk in a bowl and add into the bowl of flour.

3. Mix until well combined. Do not over beat.

4. Preheat an electric Ableskiver pan according to the manufacturer's instructions.

5. Pour ¼ teaspoon oil in each well. When the oil heat, pour batter into the cavities of the pan up to ¾.

6. Cook until both sides are golden brown. Remove the doughnuts and place in an oven to keep warm.

7. Top with butter and a sprinkle of sugar or a preserve of your choice.

Rugbrod - Scandinavian Rye Bread

Makes: 1 small loaf

Ingredients:

- ¼ cup rye berries, rinsed, drained

- ¼ cup millet, rinsed, drained

- 2 cups whole grain rye flour

- ½ envelope active dry yeast (about 1/8 ounce)

- ½ cup bread flour

- ½ cup + ¼ cup rolled oats

- 2 ½ cups + 2 tablespoons warm water

- 1 tablespoon fine sea salt

- Vegetable oil, to grease

Method:

1. Add rye into a small saucepan. Pour 1 cup water. Place over medium heat and bring to the boil.

2. Lower heat and simmer until dry and the rye berries are slightly tender. Transfer on to a sheet of parchment paper and allow it to cool.

3. Add millets into a small saucepan. Pour ½ cup water. Place over medium heat and bring to the boil.

4. Lower heat and simmer until dry and the millets are slightly tender. Transfer on to a sheet of parchment paper and allow it to cool.

5. Fit the stand mixer with the paddle. Add yeast into the bowl of the stand mixer. Pour remaining water. Let it sit for 10-15 minutes until frothy.

6. Add salt, rye flour and bread flour into the bowl. Set the mixer on low and mix for about 3-5 minutes.

7. Raise the speed to medium and mix for about 2 minutes.

8. Add millet, rye berries, and ½ cup oats. Continue mixing until well combined.

9. Place the dough into a large greased bowl. Cover the bowl cling wrap. Place it in a warm area for 2-4 hours or until it doubles in size.

10. Sprinkle remaining oats on your countertop. Place the dough on the oats and roll until the oats are coated on the dough.

11. Shape the dough into a loaf and place it in a small loaf pan. Cover the pan with a moist kitchen towel. Place in a warm area for 1 ½ - 2 hours.

12. Preheat the oven at 450° F and then bake the bread for 40-50 minutes or until light brown on top.

13. Remove the bread from the oven and place on a wire rack to cool.

14. Remove from the loaf pan and cool completely.

15. Slice and serve.

Danish Bubble

Serves: 2

Ingredients:

- 1 medium onion, finely chopped

- 1 cup leftover meat, chopped

- 1 cup cooked potatoes, cubed, cold

- 3 slices bacon, lightly cooked, chopped

- 4 tablespoons oil or butter

- 1 teaspoon Worcestershire sauce

- Salt to taste

- Pepper to taste

- 2 eggs

- 2 teaspoons butter.

- ½ cup cheddar cheese, grated

- ½ bunch chives, chopped

Method:

1. Place a skillet over medium heat. Add 1-tablespoon oil. When the oil is heated, add meat and cook until brown. Remove the meat and set aside.

2. Add 1-tablespoon oil to the skillet. Add potatoes and cook until crisp and golden brown on all the sides. Remove the potatoes and set aside.

3. Add remaining oil into the skillet. Add onions and sauté until translucent.

4. Stir in the meat, chives, bacon and potatoes. Mix well. Heat thoroughly. Sprinkle salt and pepper. Add Worcestershire sauce and stir.

5. Meanwhile, cook the eggs, sunny side up in butter.

6. Divide the bubble into 2 plates. Place egg on top. Sprinkle cheddar cheese on top and serve.

Open face Salmon and Egg Scandinavian Sandwich

Serves: 3

Ingredients:

- 2 ounces smoked salmon

- Salt to taste

- Pepper to taste

- 1 tablespoon butter, softened

- 2 eggs

- 1 sprig fresh dill, chopped

- 6 slices mini rye bread

Method:

1. Apply butter on one side of the bread slices.

2. Place a nonstick skillet over medium heat. Add eggs, salt and pepper. Scramble the eggs and cook until creamy.

3. Using a fork, flake the fish.

4. Sprinkle scrambled egg over the bread slices. Sprinkle fish and dill over the eggs.

5. Serve right away.

Hazelnut Butter & Strawberry Sandwich

Serves: 4

Ingredients:

- 4 slices rye bread

- 4 tablespoons hazelnut butter

- 4 large strawberries, sliced

- A handful fresh basil, chopped

- Honey or maple syrup, as required

- Bee pollen to sprinkle

Method:

1. Spread a tablespoon of hazelnut butter on each of the bread slices.

2. Place strawberry slices over the bread.

3. Sprinkle bee pollen and basil.

4. Trickle some honey or maple syrup on top.

5. Serve right away.

Raisin Scones

Makes: 24

Ingredients:

<u>For dry ingredients:</u>

- 4 cups flour + extra to dust
- 4 teaspoons baking powder
- 1 teaspoon baking soda
- 4 tablespoons sugar + extra to top
- 1 teaspoon salt
- 1 teaspoon ground nutmeg

<u>For wet ingredients:</u>

- 2 cups raisins
- 2 egg whites
- 1 cup cold butter, cubed
- 1 ½ cups buttermilk

Method:

1. Add all the dry ingredients into a large bowl and stir until well combined.

2. Add butter. Cut the butter into the dry ingredients using a pastry cutter until crumbly in texture.

3. Add butter and raisins. Stir until well combined.

4. Dust your countertop with a little flour. Knead the dough 6-8 times.

5. Divide the dough into 2 equal portions and pat each into a circle of about 8 inches diameter. Cut each into 12 wedges.

6. Grease a large baking sheet with a little oil or butter. Place the scones over it. Use 2 baking sheets if required and bake in batches.

7. Bake in a preheated oven at 400 °F for 15 minutes or until golden brown on top.

Biksemad - Scandinavian Hash

Serves: 2

Ingredients:

- 1.5 ounces butter

- ¾ pound cooked cold potatoes, diced

- Salt as per taste

- Pepper as per taste

- 1 medium onion, chopped

- ½ pound cooked leftover meat

- 2 fried eggs to serve (optional)

Method:

1. Place a skillet over medium heat. Add half the butter. When the butter melts, add onions and cook until it turns golden brown. Remove onions with a slotted spoon and place in a bowl. Set aside.

2. Add remaining butter into the same skillet. When the butter melts, add potatoes and cook until light brown.

3. Stir in the meat. Let it cook for a few minutes.

4. Add the onions back into the skillet. Mix well. Cook for a couple of minutes.

5. Divide into 2 plates. Place fried egg on top if using and serve.

Danish Rolls

Serves: 4

Ingredients:

<u>For rolls:</u>

- 4 ounces cream cheese, softened

- ½ tablespoon lemon juice

- 2 teaspoons lingonberry jam or any other jam of your choice

- ¼ cup sugar

- 1 can (8 ounces) refrigerated crescent dinner rolls

<u>For glaze:</u>

- ¼ cup powdered sugar

- 1-2 teaspoons milk

- ½ teaspoon vanilla extract

Method:

1. Add cream cheese, lemon juice and sugar into a bowl. Beat until creamy.

2. Make 4 rectangles of the dough by separating it out. Press on holes firmly so that it is well sealed.

3. Place the rectangles on your countertop. Take about 2 tablespoons of the cream cheese mixture and spread it evenly over the rectangles.

4. Start at the longest edge and roll the rectangles. Press the edges firmly so that it is well sealed. Slowly stretch the rolls until they are about 10 inches long.

5. Roll each of the rounds into a spiral on a baking sheet (arrange it in a coil). Do not grease the baking sheet. Leave a gap between 2 rolls. Press each of the rolls in the center to get a depression.

6. Place ½ teaspoon jam in the depression.

7. Bake in a preheated oven at 250 °F for 20-25 minutes or until golden brown on top.

8. To make glaze: Add all the glaze ingredients into a bowl and stir.

9. When the rolls are ready, remove from the oven and cool until it is warm.

10. Trickle the glaze over the rolls and serve.

Norwegian Romme Grot

Serves: 2-3

Ingredients:

- 10 ounces sour cream

- 20 ounces whole milk

- 12 ounces all-purpose flour

- 1 teaspoon salt

- Ground cinnamon, to taste

- Salted butter, to taste

- Sugar, to taste

Method:

1. Stir constantly throughout the cooking process.

2. Add sour cream into a pan. Place the pan over low heat. When sour cream melts, sprinkle a little flour at a time and whisk well each time.

3. As it starts becoming thicker, add a little milk after each addition of flour. Whisk well each time. Continue this process until all the flour and milk is added. Do not forget to stir constantly.

4. In a while it will begin to boil. Let it simmer for a couple of minutes.

5. Add butter, sugar and cinnamon and stir. Let it simmer for 2-3 minutes.

6. Ladle into bowls and serve.

Creamy Curried Egg Salad Sandwich

Serves: 4

Ingredients:

For creamy curried egg salad:

- 8 eggs, hard boiled, peeled, chopped

- 4 tablespoons mayonnaise

- 2 teaspoons curry powder

- 4 tablespoons yogurt

- Salt, as per taste

To serve:

- 8 slices rye bread

- 8 cherry tomatoes, halved

- Chopped chives to garnish

- 1 cup alfalfa sprouts

Method:

7. To make creamy curry salad: Add mayonnaise, curry powder, yogurt and salt into a bowl and stir well.

8. Add eggs and fold gently.

9. Toast the bread slices.

10. Take 8 slices of bread and place on a serving platter. Divide the egg mixture over the bread. Spread it evenly over it. Sprinkle alfalfa sprouts over it. Sprinkle chives. Place tomatoes on top and serve right away.

Scandinavian Breakfast Muesli

Serves:

Ingredients:

For muesli:

- 1 cup rolled oats

- 2 teaspoons quinoa flakes

- 4 tablespoons nuts of your choice, chopped

- 2 teaspoons flaxseeds

- 4 tablespoons unsweetened coconut flakes

- 4 tablespoons dried berries

To serve:

- Milk or yogurt

- Maple syrup

Method:

1. Add all the ingredients of muesli into a bowl and toss.

2. Transfer into an airtight container and place in a dry area.

3. To serve: Take the required amount of muesli in a bowl. Add milk or yogurt. Drizzle maple syrup on top and serve.

Ollebrod - Danish Rye Bread Porridge

Serves: 6

Ingredients:

- 1/3 cup malt syrup

- ¾ pound stale rye bread, cut into 1 inch cubes

- 1 ½ teaspoons vanilla extract

- 3 tablespoons unsalted butter

- 6 tablespoons heavy cream to serve (optional)

- 1 cup apple juice

- 12 ounces dark, malty beer

- 2 strips orange peel

- 1 ½ teaspoons ground cinnamon

- ¾ teaspoon ground cardamom

- ¼ teaspoon kosher salt or to taste

- Fresh fruits of your choice to serve (optional)

Method:

1. Place rye bread in a bowl. Pour beer over it. Cover and place it at room temperature overnight.

2. Add the bread mixture into a saucepan. Pour ¾ cup water, apple juice, malt syrup and vanilla and stir. Also add orange peel, cinnamon and cardamom and stir.

3. Place the saucepan over medium high heat.

4. When it begins to boil, lower heat and simmer for 6-7 minutes until thick. Stir occasionally. Mash the bread cubes with the back of your ladle or spoon.

5. Turn off the heat. Discard orange peels. Add butter and salt and stir until butter melts.

6. Ladle into bowls. Place a blob of cream.

7. Serve with fruits if using.

Chapter Two: Norwegian Lunch Recipes

Skagen Toast

Serves: 4

Ingredients:

- 14 ounces small prawns, peeled

- 4 tablespoons mayonnaise

- Juice of a lemon

- A handful fresh dill, chopped + extra to garnish

- Fish roe to serve

- 1 small red onion, finely chopped

- 2 tablespoons sour cream

- White Pepper, as per taste

- Brioche or sourdough, toasted

- Butter if desired

Method:

1. Add prawns, onion, sour cream, mayonnaise, salt, pepper and lemon juice into a bowl and mix well. Let it sit for 5 minutes.

2. Add dill and stir.

3. Spread over toasts. Butter the toasts if desired.

4. Place fish roe on top. Sprinkle dill and serve.

Herring Sandwiches

Serves: 3

Ingredients:

- 2 thin pickled herring fillets, cut into ½ inch pieces

- 2 tablespoons finely chopped onions

- ½ small apple, peeled, cored, cut into ¼ inch cubes

- 1 tablespoon dill pickle, finely chopped

- 1 tablespoon mayonnaise

- 2 tablespoons butter, at room temperature

- Green lettuce leaves

- 1 small potato, boiled, peeled, cut into cubes of ¼ inch

- Freshly ground Pepper, as per taste

- Salt, as per taste

- 3 thin slices black bread, halved

Method:

1. Smear butter over the bread halves. Place a lettuce leaf on each.

2. Mix together rest of the ingredients in a bowl. Spread over the lettuce leaves and serve.

Gravlax Club Sandwich

Serves: 4

Ingredients:

- 8 slices bacon, halved crosswise, cooked until crisp

- 8 thin slices grain bread, toasted

- 4 thin slices gravlax or smoked salmon

- 1 thin slice gravlax, cut into 8 strips crosswise

- 1 red onion, finely chopped

- 4 sprigs, cilantro, finely chopped

- 1 jalapeño pepper, finely chopped

- 8 mint leaves, finely chopped

- Juice of 2 limes

- 1 medium tomato, chopped into ¼ inch pieces

- 1 clove garlic, minced

- 2 avocadoes, peeled, pitted, cut into ½ inch cubes

- Salt, as per taste

- Pepper, as per taste

Method:

1. Add onion, tomato, garlic, jalapeño and herbs in a bowl. Add avocado, salt, pepper and lime juice and stir.

2. Shape each of the gravlax into a square. Spoon about a tablespoon of the mixture in the center of the gravlax. Enclose the avocado mixture by folding over the sides of the gravlax over the avocado mixture. Place each on 4 slices of bread. Place bacon half on each. Cover with the remaining bread slices.

3. Cut each into 2 triangles.

4. Roll each of the thin strips of gravlax into a rosette.

5. Place one rosette over each triangle. Place remaining bacon on top of the rossete and serve.

Scandinavian Chicken

Serves: 2

Ingredients:

- 3 broiler-fryer chicken thighs, skinless, boneless, cut into 1 inch pieces

- Pepper, as per taste

- 4 ounces mushrooms, sliced

- ¼ cup Havarti cheese, shredded

- 1 tablespoon fresh parsley, chopped

- 1 ½ tablespoons butter

- 1/3 cup onions, finely chopped

- 6 tablespoons sour cream

- 2 tablespoons fresh bread crumbs

Method:

1. Place a pan over medium high heat. Add butter. When butter melts, add chicken and cook until brown on all the sides.

2. Season with salt and pepper. Add onions and sauté until onions are translucent.

3. Stir in the mushrooms and sauté until tender.

4. Lower heat and add cheese and sour cream. Stir and let it simmer until the cheese melts completely.

5. Turn off the heat and sprinkle breadcrumbs. Stir and sprinkle parsley.

6. Serve in bowls.

Norwegian Fish Cakes with Dill Mayonnaise

Serves: 6

Ingredients:

- 10 ounces hake fillet, skinless, cut into ½ inch pieces

- Kosher salt to taste

- Black pepper to taste

- Freshly ground white pepper to taste

- ½ tablespoon baking powder

- 7 tablespoons heavy cream

- ½ cup mayonnaise

- ½ tablespoon distilled vinegar

- 3 tablespoons unsalted butter

- 2 tablespoons fresh dill, chopped + extra to garnish

Method:

1. Add hake into the food processor and process until it is minced.

2. Add baking powder, black pepper and about a teaspoon salt and process until well combined.

3. With the food processor running, pour cream through the feeder tube and process until smooth and light to touch.

4. Place a large nonstick skillet over medium heat. Add half the butter. Place about ¼ cup of the cake mixture on the skillet. Press until it is ½ inch in thickness. Similarly, make some more cakes.

5. Cook until it gets golden brown on both sides. Remove the fish cakes and keep it warm.

6. Repeat the above 2 steps to make the remaining butter and mixture.

7. To make dill mayonnaise: Add dill, vinegar, mayonnaise, salt and pepper into a bowl and mix well.

8. Serve warm fish cakes with dill mayonnaise. Sprinkle some more dill on top and serve.

Danish Glazed Mushrooms

Serves: 2-3

- **Ingredients:**
- ½ pound mushroom caps
- ¼ teaspoon salt
- 1 ½ tablespoons olive oil
- ¼ teaspoon paprika
- 1 small green onion, chopped
- 1 small clove garlic, crushed
- ½ tablespoon fresh dill, chopped
- A handful fresh parsley, chopped
- 1 teaspoon dried basil

Method:

1. Place a nonstick skillet over medium high heat. Add oil. When the oil is heated, add garlic, green onion, paprika and salt.

2. Sauté until the mushrooms are tender.

3. Add herbs and toss well.

4. Serve right away.

Potato Pancakes

Serves: 2

Ingredients:

- 1 cup grated raw potatoes

- 1 egg, beaten

- ¼ teaspoon salt

- 1 small onion, grated

- ¼ cup sifted flour

Method:

1. Add all the ingredients into a bowl and mix until well combined.

2. Place a pan over medium heat. Place half the mixture on the pan. Spread slightly.

3. Cook until it gets golden brown on both sides. Remove on to a plate.

4. Repeat the above 2 steps with the remaining mixture.

5. Serve right away.

Blue Cheese, Pear, and Hazelnut Smørrebrød

Serves: 2

Ingredients:

- 4 tablespoons Danish blue cheese, crushed

- 2 slices rugbrod (rye bread) of 1/3 inch each, trimmed

- ½ pear, cored, peeled, thinly sliced lengthwise

- 4 teaspoons toasted hazelnuts, chopped

- 1 teaspoon unsalted butter, at room temperature

Method:

1. Apply butter on one side of the bread slice.

2. Place pear slices on the bread slices, overlapping each other.

3. Sprinkle blue cheese and hazelnuts.

4. Serve immediately.

Shrimp Egg and Dill Smorrebrod

Serves: 2

Ingredients:

- 2 slices rye bread (¼ inch thick)

- 1 thin slice rye bread for breadcrumbs

- 10-12 tiny shrimp, cooked, defrost if frozen

- Salt to taste

- Freshly ground pepper to taste

- 3 small eggs, hard boiled, peeled, cut into half inch thick slices

- ½ tablespoon Dijon mustard

- Small dill sprigs or finely chopped chives to garnish

- 2 -3 tablespoons dill mayonnaise – refer Fish cakes with Dill mayonnaise recipe

Method:

1. Toast the bread in a preheated oven 300 °F until dry and crisp.

2. When done, crumble into smaller pieces.

3. Add shrimp and mustard into a bowl and stir.

4. To assemble: Place the bread slices on a serving platter. Spread 1-1 ½ tablespoons dill mayonnaise on it.

5. Sprinkle salt. Place egg slices over the bread. Sprinkle salt and pepper.

6. Place 4-5 shrimp on each slice. Sprinkle breadcrumbs, dill and pepper.

7. Serve right away.

Venison Sandwich with Bacon, Chestnut Crème Fraiche and Lingonberry jam

Serves: 4

Ingredients:

- 4 teaspoons juniper berries
- 1 teaspoon black peppercorns
- 2 teaspoons pink peppercorns
- 1.7 pounds venison loin
- 8 rashers smoked streaky bacon, cooked until crisp
- 4 teaspoons allspice
- 2 teaspoons salt
- 3 tablespoons butter
- 2 multi-seed loaves, sliced, toasted
- 8 rashers smoked streaky bacon
- 2 drops rapeseed oil

For lingonberry jam:

- 6-7 tablespoons sugar or to taste
- 1.1 pounds lingonberries or cranberries

For chestnut crème fraiche:

- 21 ounces crème fraiche

- 1.7 ounces chestnuts

Method:

1. Add allspice, juniper berries, black and pink peppercorns into a spice grinder and grind until smooth.

2. Add salt and mix well.

3. Rub this spice mixture all over the venison loin.

4. Place an ovenproof pan over medium heat. Add butter and rapeseed oil.

5. When butter melts, add meat and cook until brown on both the sides.

6. Transfer the pan into a preheated oven.

7. Bake at 325 °F for 7-10 minutes.

8. Remove the pan and wrap with foil. Let it sit for 15 minutes.

9. Cut into thin slices.

10. Meanwhile, make the lingonberry jam as follows: Add lingonberries and sugar into a skillet. Place the skillet over medium low heat. Cook for 7-8 minutes. Turn off the heat.

11. To make chestnut crème fraiche: Add chestnut and cream fraiche into a blender and blend until smooth.

12. Spread chestnut crème fraiche on one side of the toasted bread slices.

13. Top with venison slices and bacon.

14. Drizzle lingonberry jam on top and serve.

Lindström Patties

Serves: 2-3

Ingredients:

- 9 ounces minced beef

- White pepper to taste

- 1 egg yolk

- 1 ½ tablespoons pickled gherkins, finely chopped

- 2 ½ tablespoons pickled beetroots, finely chopped

- Freshly grated horseradish to serve

- Chives, chopped, to serve

- ½ teaspoon salt

- 1.7 ounces water

- 1 tablespoons capers, chopped

- Butter, to fry

Method:

1. Add beef, salt and pepper into a bowl and stir.

2. Add water, yolk, gherkins, beets and capers and stir.

3. Divide the mixture into 2-3 portions and shape into patties.

4. Place a skillet on the stove and turn the heat to medium. Add a little butter. Place the patties on the skillet and cook until they are golden brown on both sides.

5. Serve topped with horseradish and chives. Drizzle the cooked liquid if any on top and serve.

Chapter Three: Norwegian Dinner Recipes

Sautéed Chicken with Caraway and Cream

Serves: 3

Ingredients:

- 3 whole chicken breasts, skinless, boneless, cut into ½ inch wide strips

- 5 white mushrooms, sliced

- ½ ounces morel or any other dried mushrooms, soaked in hot water for 30 minutes, drained, roughly chopped

- 3 shallots, minced

- ¼ cup vegetable oil

- 1 cup madeira

- 1 tablespoon caraway seeds, chopped

- 2 cups chicken stock

- ¼ teaspoon salt

- Hot sauce to taste

- 1 cup heavy cream

- Freshly ground Pepper, as per taste

- Wide egg noodles, cooked, to serve

Method:

1. Sprinkle salt and pepper over the chicken strips and place in a bowl. Drizzle a tablespoon of oil and toss until well combined.

2. Place a pan over high flame. Add 3 tablespoons oil. When the oil is heated, add chicken and cook until done or it gets a nice golden brown tint on the outside and pink inside. It should take about a minute on each side. Remove the chicken strips with a slotted spoon and set aside.

3. Place the pan back over heat. Add shallots and sliced mushrooms and cook until tender.

4. Stir in caraway seeds and sauté for 30-60 seconds until fragrant. Remove the pan off the heat.

5. Stir in Madeira and place it back over high heat. Boil until it is reduced to half its original quantity.

6. Add stock, soaked mushrooms and cream. Let it cook until the sauce is thickened as per your desire.

7. Lower heat. Add chicken along with the cooked juices, salt and pepper and stir.

8. Heat thoroughly.

9. Serve over wide egg noodles.

Scandinavian Chicken and Cabbage

Serves: 2-3

Ingredients:

- 2 tablespoons vegetable oil

- 4 chicken legs

- 14 ounces canned, chopped tomatoes with its juices

- 1 small onion, chopped

- 2 cups cabbage, shredded

- ¼ cup all-purpose flour

- ½ teaspoon celery seeds

- 1 teaspoon caraway seeds

- ½ teaspoon seasoning salt

- ½ teaspoon sugar

- ½ teaspoon sugar

- ½ cup mozzarella cheese, shredded

Method:

1. Place a skillet over high heat. Add oil and let it heat.

2. Meanwhile, sprinkle flour, seasoned salt and celery seeds into a zip lock bag. Place chicken legs in it and shake the bag so that the chicken is coated with the mixture.

3. Place chicken in the heated skillet. Cook until brown on all the sides. Remove chicken with a slotted spoon ad place in a baking dish.

4. Add onions into the same skillet. Sauté until translucent.

5. Stir in tomatoes, sugar, caraway seeds and sugar. When it begins to boil, add cabbage and stir. Turn off the heat and spread over the chicken in the baking dish. Cover the baking dish with aluminum foil.

6. Bake in a preheated oven at 350 °F for 20-25 minutes.

7. Uncover and sprinkle cheese over it. Bake for another 5-7 minutes.

8. Serve hot or warm.

Chicken with Rosemary and Juniper

Serves: 2

Ingredients:

- 2 chicken breast fillets, scored

- 8 Bart juniper berries, ground

- ½ teaspoon corn starch

- 1/3 cup hot vegetable or chicken stock

- 1 tablespoon fresh rosemary, finely chopped

- ½ tablespoon olive oil

- 1/3 cup half fat crème fraiche

- Brown basmati rice or wild rice to serve

- Salad leaves to serve

- Salt, as per taste

- Pepper, as per taste

Method:

1. Place chicken in a roasting pan. Sprinkle rosemary and juniper berries over it.

2. Sprinkle salt and pepper over it. Drizzle ½ tablespoon olive oil over the chicken.

3. Bake in a preheated oven at 350 °F for 20 minutes.

4. Add cornstarch and crème fraiche in a bowl. Add stock and stir. Pour over the chicken.

5. Bake for another 15 minutes or until the chicken is cooked.

6. Serve over brown basmati rice and a green salad.

Norwegian Chicken Braised with Dried Fruit

Serves: 2

Ingredients:

- 2 tablespoons butter or oil

- 1 small onion, chopped

- 1 ½ pounds fryer chicken

- 1 teaspoon dried thyme

- 1 cup stock or water

- Salt, as per taste

- Pepper, as per taste

- Few thin slices lemon

- 1 cup assorted dried fruit

Method:

1. Place a Dutch oven over medium heat. Add butter. When butter melts, add chicken and cook until brown. Remove with a slotted spoon and place on a plate.

2. Add onions into the Dutch oven and sauté until translucent.

3. Add the chicken back into the pot and 1-½ cups of water. Add salt, pepper and thyme.

4. When it begins to boil, lower heat and cover with a lid. Simmer for 15 minutes.

5. Add dried fruit and stir. Place chicken slices on top. Sprinkle salt and pepper.

6. Cover and cook until the chicken is cooked and not pink anymore.

Fried Herring Pickled in Liquor

Serves: 4-5

Ingredients:

- 4 whole herring, cut open in the middle

- 1 medium carrot, thinly sliced

- 1 small onion, thinly sliced crosswise

- White pepper powder to taste

- Kosher Salt, as per taste

- 2-3 tablespoons Dijon mustard

- 4 tablespoons unsalted butter

- 1 tablespoon parsley, minced

- 1 tablespoon dill, minced

- 1 cup sugar

- 1 bay leaf

- 5 whole allspice berries

- 1 ¼ cups distilled white vinegar

- 3 whole white peppercorns

- 5 whole black peppercorns

- Rye toast to serve

- Boiled potatoes to serve

Method:

1. Place herrings on your countertop with the flesh facing up. Each one should be opened like a book.

2. Sprinkle salt and white pepper on top. Smear mustard on top with a brush.

3. Sprinkle herbs and close each like a book in such a manner that the flesh touches each other.

4. Place a large nonstick skillet over medium heat. Add butter. When butter melts, add fillets and cook until the underside (skin side) is light brown. Flip sides and cook the other side until light brown. Cook in batches if required.

5. Remove the fillets and place on a plate lined with blotting paper. After a while place the fillets in a baking dish in one layer, without overlapping.

6. Meanwhile, place a saucepan over medium heat. Add sugar and ¾ cup water and stir. Bring to the boil. Stir frequently. When sugar dissolves, turn off the heat.

7. Add carrot, onion, vinegar and spices. Stir and pour over the fillets. Let it cool completely.

8. Cover the baking dish with cling wrap and chill for 12-15 hours.

9. To serve: Remove the fillets from the dish and place on a plate. Spoon a little of the pickling liquid over it. Serve with boiled potatoes and rye toast.

Pike Perch with Creamed Mushrooms and Horseradish Butter

Serves: 8

Ingredients:

- 4 ½ sticks unsalted butter

- 2 ½ pounds pike-perch or walleye fillets, skin-on

- 3 ½ pounds crimini mushrooms, halved

- Kosher Salt, as per taste

- White pepper powder to taste

- Freshly ground black Pepper, as per taste

- 1 cup prepared horseradish or 8 ounces horseradish, finely grated

- ¼ cup flat leaf parsley, chopped

- 1 cup plain breadcrumbs

- ¼ cup heavy cream

Method:

1. Place a large skillet over medium heat. Add 4 tablespoons butter. When butter melts, stir in the mushroom and cook for 4 minutes. Do not stir during these 4 minutes.

2. Stir occasionally and cook until light brown for another 4 minutes. Cook in batches if required.

3. Add salt and white pepper powder and stir.

4. Add 4 tablespoons butter and cream and stir. Turn off the heat. Cover and set aside.

5. Place a saucepan over medium heat. Add 2 sticks butter. When butter melts, add horseradish and stir. Cover the saucepan with a lid and remove from heat. Set aside.

6. Place another large skillet over medium high heat. Add 1 stick of butter. Let it melt.

7. Sprinkle salt and black pepper over the fillets. Now sprinkle breadcrumbs evenly over the fillets.

8. Place a few fillets with the skin side facing down. Cook until done or it gets a golden brown tint. Flip sides and cook until done. Remove the fillets and place on a plate lined with paper towels.

9. Repeat the above 3 steps with the remaining fillets.

10. Place mushrooms on a serving platter. Sprinkle parsley over it. Place the fillets with the skin side facing on top.

11. Place horseradish butter on top and serve right away.

Pasta with Crayfish

Serves: 4

Ingredients:

- 12 ounces dried pasta like penne pasta

- 2 tablespoons butter

- ½ cup white wine

- Zest of 2 lemons, grated

- Juice of 1 lemon

- 12 ounces crayfish tails

- 1 lemon, quartered, to garnish

- 1 large onion, thinly sliced

- 2 teaspoons cornstarch

- 1 ½ cups half fat crème fraiche

- Salt, as per taste

- White Pepper, as per taste

- ¼ cup dill, finely chopped

- 4 small sprigs dill to garnish

Method:

1. Cook pasta following the directions on the package. Drain and set aside.

2. Place a skillet over medium heat. Add butter. When butter melts, add onions and sauté until translucent.

3. Stir in the cornstarch for a few seconds. Pour wine and crème fraiche and whisk until well combined.

4. Lower heat and let it simmer for 5-7 minutes. Stir frequently. Turn off the heat.

5. Add lemon juice, salt and pepper. Taste and adjust the lemon juice and salt and pepper if necessary.

6. Add crayfish tails and chopped dill. Mix well. Transfer most of the crayfish tail mixture into the bowl of pasta. Toss well.

7. Serve in individual bowls. Top with remaining crayfish tail mixture and lemon zest.

8. Place a sprig of dill and lemon quarter in each bowl. Top with radish slices if desired.

9. Serve with salad.

Roast Pork Loin with Salted Caramel Potatoes

Serves: 4

Ingredients:

- 1 ½ - 2 pounds pork loin roast, skin-on

- 3 medium yellow onions, halved

- ½ bunch thyme

- ½ pound fingerling potatoes

- 4 tablespoons unsalted butter

- Freshly ground black Pepper, as per taste

- Red currant jelly, to serve

- Kosher Salt, as per taste

- 2 fresh bay leaves

- 1 tablespoon olive oil

- ¼ cup sugar

- Flaky sea Salt, as per taste

- ½ teaspoon apple cider vinegar

Method:

1. Take a sharp knife and score the pork roast on the skin, crosswise. Do this every ¼ inch of the pork. Do not cut inside the fat, cut only the skin.

2. Sprinkle salt and pepper all over the skin especially on the scored area. Rub the salt and pepper into the skin on the score.

3. Spread onions in a roasting pan.

4. Sprinkle bay leaves and thyme over it. Place a roasting rack over the onions.

5. Place the pork roast, with its skin side facing down over the rack.

6. Pour 3-4 cups boiling water in the roasting pan.

7. Place pan in a preheated oven.

8. Bake in a preheated oven at 350 °F for 40-50 minutes or until the internal temperature of the pork is 140 °F. It might take longer to cook. Turn the pork roast half way through baking.

9. When the pork is done, broil for the last 3-5 minutes until the skin is crisp.

10. Remove the pork and place on your cutting board. Cover the pork with foil and let it sit for some time.

11. Meanwhile make the potatoes as follows: Place a saucepan half-filled with water over medium heat.

12. When the water begins to boil, add potatoes and cook until tender. Discard the water and set the potatoes aside for a while to cool.

13. When cool enough to handle, peel the potatoes.

14. Place a medium skillet over medium high heat. Add sugar and 2-3 tablespoons water.

15. Swirl the skillet frequently. In a while the sugar will begin to caramelize.

16. When the sugar turns into a nice golden brown color, add potatoes and butter and stir until well coated.

17. Cook for about 20 minutes. The potatoes will be sticky to touch. Sprinkle salt and pepper and stir. Turn off the heat.

18. When the pork is cool enough to handle, slice the pork.

19. Pass the cooked juices that are in the roasting pan through a fine wire mesh strainer that is placed over a bowl. Remove the fat that is floating on top.

20. Add vinegar, salt and pepper and stir.

21. Serve pork with the cooked liquid poured on top along with red currant jelly placed on the side as well as caramel potatoes.

Wiener schnitzel

Serves: 4

Ingredients:

- ¼ cup all-purpose flour

- 1 cup dried breadcrumbs

- 4 veal scaloppine (3.5 ounces each)

- 3 large eggs, lightly beaten

- ½ cup clarified butter or ghee

- Kosher Salt, as per taste

- Freshly ground white Pepper, as per taste

To serve: Use any or all of them, as required

- Salt packed capers

- Anchovies

- Horseradish, freshly grated

- Lemon wedges

Method:

1. Pound veal scaloppine with a meat mallet until it is ¼ inch thick.

2. Place flour in a shallow bowl. Place breadcrumbs in another shallow bowl. Place egg in a 3rd shallow bowl.

3. Sprinkle salt and pepper over the veal scaloppine.

4. First dredge the scaloppine in flour. Shake to drop off excess flour.

5. Next dip in eggs. Shake to drop off excess eggs.

6. Finally dredge in breadcrumbs and place on a wire rack.

7. Place a large skillet over medium high heat. Add 1-tablespoon ghee. When it melts, place 1 scaloppine and cook until done or it gets a golden brown tint. Flip sides and add another tablespoon of ghee. Cook until golden brown. Remove scaloppine with a slotted spoon and place on a plate that is lined with paper towels.

8. Repeat the above step with the remaining scaloppine.

9. To assemble: Place one scaloppine on each serving plate. Place 1-2 anchovies over it. Sprinkle capers. Place some horseradish on top. Serve with lemon wedges.

Scandinavian Meatballs with Mash and Lingon Sauce

Serves: 3

Ingredients:

<u>For meatballs:</u>

- 1.1 pounds minced pork or veal or a combination of both

- 2 ounces cream

- 1 small onion, minced

- 2 tablespoons dried breadcrumbs

- A pinch grated nutmeg

- A pinch allspice

- 2 tablespoons oil, to fry

<u>For red wine sauce:</u>

- ½ cup beef stock or wild mushroom stock

- 1 tablespoon plain flour

- 8 tablespoons red wine

- ½ tablespoon caster sugar

- 1 clove garlic, finely sliced

- 2 tablespoons butter

- ½ teaspoon soy sauce

- ½ teaspoon thyme leaves, chopped

- Freshly ground Pepper, as per taste

- Salt, as per taste

To serve:

- Mashed potatoes

- Lingonberry sauce

Method:

1. To make meatballs: Add all the ingredients except oil into a bowl and mix until well combined.

2. Divide the mixture into tablespoon size portions. Shape into balls.

3. Place a skillet over medium heat. Add oil. When the oil is heated, add meatballs and cook until brown on all the sides. Remove with a slotted spoon and place on a plate that is lined with paper towels.

4. To make red wine sauce: Add flour to the same skillet. Stir for about a minute. Scrape the bottom of the skillet to remove any brown bits that are stuck.

5. Add rest of the ingredients except butter and stir. Stir constantly until it thickens. Add a little water if you like the taste diluted. Add butter and stir. Taste and adjust the seasoning if required. Use as much as required and store the rest in an airtight container in the refrigerator. It can last for 2-3 days.

6. Add meatballs and stir until the meatballs are well coated. Let it simmer until it is cooked.

7. Serve on individual serving plate with mashed potatoes and lingonberry sauce on the side.

Swedish Meat Pies

Serves: 8

Ingredients:

- 2 pounds ground beef, crumbled

- 2 tablespoons butter

- ½ cup onion, chopped

- ½ teaspoon ground allspice

- 1/8 teaspoon ground nutmeg

- ½ teaspoons dried dill weed

- ¼ cup fresh parsley, chopped

- 4 large red potatoes, grated

- 4 cups all-purpose flour

- 1 ½ cups shortening

- 4 cups cheddar cheese

- 2 teaspoons salt

- ¾ cup sour cream

Method:

1. Place a large skillet over medium heat. Add butter. When butter melts, add beef, spices, parsley, onion, dill and potatoes and cook until beef is brown.

2. Drain off any extra fat remaining in the pan. Remove from heat.

3. Add cheese and stir. Set aside for a while.

4. Meanwhile, make the piecrust as follows: Add flour and salt in a bowl. Add shortening and cut with a pastry cutter until crumbs of pea size are formed.

5. Add sour cream, a little at a time and mix well each time. Eventually dough has to form.

6. Dust your countertop with a little flour and knead the dough. Make 8 equal portions of the dough and shape into balls.

7. Roll the balls into rounds of 1/8-inch thickness. Place about ½ cup of filling on one half of the round. Fold the other half over. The filling. Moisten the edges with warm water and press to seal.

8. Place the pies on a baking sheet.

9. Bake in a preheated oven at 350 °F for 20 minutes or until golden brown.

10. Cool for a while and serve.

Biff stroganoff - Beef stroganoff

Serves: 4

Ingredients:

- 18 ounces beef (fillet or sirloin or rump), cut into strips of about ½ inch width

- 2 small onions, thinly sliced

- 14 ounces mixed wild mushrooms, sliced

- 2 tablespoons brandy or sherry (optional)

- 6 tablespoons butter

- ½ teaspoon freshly ground pepper or to taste

- 1 cup sour cream

- Salt, as per taste

Method:

1. Place a large skillet over medium heat.

2. Add 2 tablespoons butter. When butter melts, add half the beef. Sprinkle salt and pepper. Raise the heat to medium - high heat and sauté until brown on both the sides. It will get brown quickly.

3. Remove with a slotted spoon and set aside.

4. Repeat step 2 to brown the remaining beef.

5. Lower heat to medium heat. Add 1 tablespoon of butter. When butter melts, add onions and sauté until translucent. Transfer into the bowl of beef.

6. Add 1 tablespoon of butter. When butter melts, add mushrooms and raise the heat to high heat. Add salt, pepper and nutmeg. Stir occasionally and cook until tender.

7. Lower heat and sour cream and mix well. Turn off the heat the moment sour cream is warm.

8. Add beef and onions and mix well. Taste and adjust the seasoning if required. Add brandy if using and stir.

9. Serve.

Lammstek med Timjan-rödvinsås -Roast Lamb with Thyme and Red Wine Sauce

Serves: 8

Ingredients:

- 4 pounds leg of lamb, boneless, trimmed of fat

- 4 teaspoons fresh rosemary leaves, finely chopped

- 4 teaspoons fresh thyme leaves, chopped

- Zest of 2 lemons, grated

- 1 tablespoon butter

- 1 tablespoon oil

- Black peppercorns, crushed, to taste

For red wine sauce: Refer Scandinavian meatballs recipe

Method:

1. Chop the lamb into smaller joints. Fasten with a string if required.

2. Sprinkle lamb joints with pepper, fresh herbs and lemon zest.

3. Place a large skillet over medium heat. Add butter. When butter melts, add lamb and cook until brown.

4. Transfer into a roasting pan.

5. Bake in a preheated oven at 250 °F for 30 minutes or until the internal temperature reaches 140 °F.

6. Remove the roasting pan from the oven and let it sit for a while.

7. Make red wine sauce following the recipe in Scandinavian meatballs with mashed potatoes and lingonberry sauce.

8. When lamb is cool enough to handle, slice the lamb. Spoon some red wine sauce on top. Sprinkle rosemary leaves and thyme flowers and serve with some more sauce.

Creamed Spinach with Crumbled Egg Yolks

Serves: 12

Ingredients:

- 6 eggs, hardboiled, peeled

- 2 large onions, chopped (about 3 cups)

- 6 tablespoons dry white vermouth

- 2 ½ pounds spinach, trimmed, chopped

- ¾ cup unsalted butter

- 2 teaspoons kosher salt, divided

- 2 cups Italian parsley leaves

- 1 ½ cups cold heavy cream

- Freshly ground Pepper, as per taste

- ½ teaspoon nutmeg, freshly grated

Method:

1. Remove the yolks from the boiled eggs. Crumble and add into a bowl. Use the whites in some other recipe.

2. Place a large saucepan over medium heat. Add butter. When butter melts, add onions and half the salt. Cook until light brown on the edges.

3. Add vermouth and stir. Increase the heat to high heat. Let it boil until most of the liquid dries off.

4. Stir in spinach, parsley and remaining salt and cook until spinach is tender.

5. Place cream in a large bowl. Remove spinach with tongs and shake to drop off excess moisture. Place spinach in the bowl of cream.

6. Stir and transfer into a blender. Blend until smooth. Pour into a bowl. Sprinkle yolks on top and serve.

Scandinavian Mashed Potato and Rutabaga Casserole

Serves: 6

Ingredients:

- 1 pound thin skinned boiling potatoes

- ½ pound rutabaga, peeled, cut into 1 inch pieces

- 1 egg

- ¼ - ½ cup hot milk or light cream

- 2 tablespoons fine dry breadcrumbs

- Salt, as per taste

- 2 tablespoons flour

- 1 teaspoon salt

- ½ tablespoon butter, chopped

Method:

1. Place potatoes in a pot. Pour enough water to cover the potatoes. Add a teaspoon of salt for every 4 cups of water.

2. Place the pot over medium heat. Cook until tender. Drain and mash the potatoes.

3. Add rutabaga. Pour enough water to cover the rutabaga. Place over medium heat. Cook until tender. Drain and mash and add into the bowl of potatoes.

4. Using an electric mixer beat until creamy.

5. Add flour, egg, milk and salt and beat until well combined.

6. Transfer the mixture into a greased baking dish. Spread it evenly. Make a few depressions all over the mixture.

7. Place butter at different spots on the mixture. Sprinkle breadcrumbs on top.

8. Bake in a preheated oven at 350 °F for 30-45 minutes or until the top is light brown.

Vegetables Au Gratin

Serves: 6

Ingredients:

- 3 large potatoes, peeled, sliced

- ¾ - 1 eggplant, sliced

- 1 medium courgette, sliced

- 6 tomatoes, sliced

- 1 ½ vegetable stock cubes

- 1/3 cup chives, chopped

- 10.5 ounces Jarlsberg cheese, grated

- Salt, as per taste

- Pepper, as per taste

Method:

1. Pour cream in a saucepan. Place over medium heat and bring to the boil.

2. Stir in the stock cubes. Stir in salt, pepper and chives. Add half the cheese and stir.

3. Place the vegetables in a greased baking dish, in layers. Spread sauce on top. Sprinkle remaining cheese on it.

4. Place rack in the center of the oven.

5. Bake in a preheated oven at 350 °F for 30-45 minutes or until the top is light brown.

Vegan Kjottkaker – Lentil Cakes with Gravy

Serves: 6

Ingredients:

- 1 ½ cups lentils

- ½ teaspoon pepper powder

- ½ teaspoon ground ginger

- ½ teaspoon ground nutmeg

- 10 teaspoons cornstarch or potato starch

- 2 teaspoons sea salt

- 1 ¼ cups soy milk, unsweetened

- Vegan butter to fry

<u>For gravy:</u>

- 3 cups soy milk, unsweetened

- Salt, as per taste

- Pepper, as per taste

- 3-4 tablespoons cornstarch

- 3 tablespoons onions, finely chopped

<u>To serve:</u>

- Boiled potatoes

- Boiled peas

- Lingonberry sauce

Method:

1. Add lentils into a pot. Add about 5-6 cups water and bring to the boil.

2. Lower heat and cover with a lid. Simmer until soft. When done, drain all the extra water from the lentils.

3. Transfer the lentils into the food processor. Also add all the spices, salt and cornstarch and process until well combined. You may end up with a paste but that is fine.

4. Transfer the paste into a bowl. Add soymilk, a little at a time. All the soymilk may not be required so add a little at a time.

5. Divide the mixture into 10-12 portions and shape into patties.

6. Place a nonstick skillet over medium heat. Add 1-2 tablespoons vegan butter. When butter melts, place a few of the patties.

7. Cook until the underside is done or it gets a golden brown tint. Flip sides and cook the other side too. Remove and set aside. Cook the remaining patties in batches.

8. To make gravy: Pour soy milk into a saucepan. Place the saucepan over medium heat. When it begins to boil, lower the cooked patties in the milk.

9. Lower heat and simmer for 10-12 minutes. Remove the patties with a slotted spoon and set aside.

10. Mix a tablespoon of water with cornstarch and pour into the simmering milk.

11. Also add onion, salt and pepper and stir constantly until thick.

12. Serve the cooked lentils with sauce spooned on top along with boiled potatoes and peas along with lingonberry sauce.

Onion Pie with Jarlsberg and Thyme

Serves: 8

Ingredients:

- 8-10 red onions, cut into ½ inch slices

- 2 bay leaves

- 6 whole cloves

- 10 black peppercorns

- 2 sheets puff pastry, thaw if frozen

- 4 teaspoons fresh thyme leaves, chopped

- 2 cups Jarlsberg cheese or any other cheese of your choice

- Salt, as per taste

Method:

1. Place a large skillet over medium high heat. Add butter. When butter melts, stir in the onions, garlic and the whole spices.

2. Lower heat to medium low and sauté until onions are very light brown. Add salt and stir. Turn off the heat.

3. Take a baking dish and place the puff pastry sheets on it. Keep it in 2 separate baking dishes if desired. Roll the pastry if necessary to fit it into the baking dish.

4. Discard the whole spices. Spread the onions over the puff pastry sheets. Sprinkle cheese and half the thyme.

5. Place the rack on the lowest level in the oven. Place the baking dish in the oven.

6. Bake in a preheated oven at 400 °F for 15 minutes or until golden brown.

7. Sprinkle remaining thyme leaves and serve.

8. Slice and serve.

Scandinavian Noodles

Serves: 6

Ingredients:

- 1 large carrot, peeled, cut into matchsticks

- Freshly ground Pepper, as per taste

- Salt, as per taste

- 2 teaspoons fresh dill or 1 teaspoon dried dill weed, chopped

- ¾ pound fine (thin) egg noodles

- 7 -8 tablespoons butter

Method:

1. Cook noodles following the directions on the package. Drain and set aside.

2. Place a skillet over medium heat. Add 3 tablespoons butter. When butter melts, add carrots, salt and pepper and sauté for a couple of minutes until the carrots are crisp as well as slightly tender.

3. Add noodles and toss well. Add dill and rest of the butter and toss well.

4. Serve right away.

Pumpkin Soup with Orange and Reggiano

Serves: 4

Ingredients:

- 1 ¼ - 1 ½ pounds sugar pumpkin or butternut squash, tr. halved lengthwise

- Kosher salt to taste

- Freshly ground pepper to taste

- 1 medium yellow onion, thinly sliced

- 3 cups vegetable stock

- Zest of ½ orange, finely grated

- Juice of ½ orange

- 3 tablespoons extra-virgin olive oil

- 2 cloves garlic, minced

- 1 small Fresno chili or red jalapeño, deseeded, finely chopped

- ½ cup crème fraiche + extra to garnish

- Parmigiano reggiano, grated, as required, to serve

Method:

1. Remove the seeds of the pumpkin and place in a bowl. Remove the strings from the seeds and rinse well. Drain and set aside on layers of paper towel. Cut the pumpkin halves into wedges and place on a baking sheet.

79

Drizzle 1 and ½ tablespoons oil over the wedges. Sprinkle salt and pepper.

3. Bake in a preheated oven at 350 °F for 30-40 minutes or until tender.

4. Remove from the oven and cool.

5. Lower the temperature of the oven to 300 °F.

6. Drizzle ½ tablespoon oil over the pumpkin seeds. Sprinkle salt and pepper. Toss well.

7. Place the pumpkin seeds on a small baking sheet.

8. Bake until the seeds are crisp.

9. Meanwhile, place a saucepan over medium heat. Add remaining oil into the pan.

10. When the oil is heated, add onion, garlic and chili and sauté until onions are translucent.

11. Discard the skin from the pumpkin and add pulp into the saucepan.

12. Add stock and stir. Bring to the boil.

13. Lower heat and simmer until slightly thick. Stir occasionally. It should take 20-25 minutes. Turn off the heat.

14. Blend with an immersion blender until smooth.

15. Place the saucepan back over low heat.

16. Add orange juice, zest, crème fraiche and stir. Turn off the heat when the soup is quite warm.

17. Add salt and pepper and stir.

18. Ladle into soup bowls. Sprinkle toasted pumpkin seeds and cheese. Place a blob of crème fraiche and serve.

Celery Root, Carrot and Potato Gratin

Serves: 4

Ingredients:

- 1 cup heavy cream

- 2 fresh bay leaves

- 2 large carrots, peeled, cut into half inch thick slices

- 1 medium yellow onion, sliced lengthwise

- 1 tablespoon fresh thyme leaves, chopped

- 2.5 ounces Gruyere cheese, grated

- 4 tablespoons unsalted butter

- 4 cloves garlic, peeled, crushed

- 2 large Russet potatoes, peeled, cut into half inch thick slices, crosswise

- ½ small celery root, peeled, cut into half inch thick slices, crosswise

- Kosher salt to taste

- Freshly ground pepper

- 1 cup fresh breadcrumbs

Method:

19. Place a saucepan over medium high heat. Add cream, butter and bay leaf.

20. When the mixture heats, add garlic and all the vegetables and bring to the boil.

21. Lower heat and simmer until vegetables are tender.

22. Turn off the heat. Add thyme and stir.

23. Transfer into a baking dish. Sprinkle salt and pepper.

24. Mix together in a bowl, cheese and bread crumbs. Sprinkle this mixture over the vegetables in the baking dish.

25. Bake in a preheated oven at 350 °F for 30-40 minutes or until golden brown on top.

26. Serve hot.

Cod with Potatoes and Sundried Tomato Pesto

Serves: 2

Ingredients:

- ¾ pound small white potatoes, halved

- 2 rosemary sprigs

- ½ cup sundried tomatoes

- 2 cloves garlic, peeled

- ¼ teaspoon sugar

- ½ cup arugula

- 3 tablespoons almonds, slivered, toasted

- 5 tablespoons olive oil

- Kosher salt to taste

- Freshly ground pepper to taste

- ½ tablespoon tomato puree

- 3 large basil leaves

- 2 cod fillets (4 ounces each)

- ¾ ounce parmesan cheese, shaved with a peeler

Method:

1. Add potatoes, 1-tablespoon oil, rosemary sprig, 1 clove garlic, salt and pepper into a baking dish. Toss well.

2. Roast in a preheated oven at 325 °F for 20 minutes or until tender.

83

3. To make pesto: Add sundried tomatoes, 1 clove garlic, tomato puree, basil and sugar into a blender and blend until smooth.

4. With the motor running, pour 3 tablespoons oil in a thin steam through the feeder tube and blend until smooth.

5. Add salt and pepper and blend again. Transfer into a bowl.

6. Place a skillet over medium heat. Add 1 tablespoon of the pesto, potatoes and 3-4 tablespoons water and stir until the potatoes are well coated with the pesto. Transfer into a bowl and keep warm.

7. Place a medium skillet with 1-tablespoon olive oil over medium heat. Season the cod fillets with salt and pepper and place on the skillet. Cook for 4 minutes. Flip sides and cook for another 3-4 minutes.

8. Divide the potatoes equally among 2 serving plates. Place a fillet on each.

9. Sprinkle arugula, Parmesan shaving and almond flakes and serve.

Swedish Turkey Meatballs

Serves: 3

Ingredients:

- 1 pound 7% lean ground turkey

- 6 tablespoons breadcrumbs

- 1 teaspoon lemon pepper seasoning

- ¼ teaspoon ground nutmeg

- ½ tablespoon onion flakes

- 1-1 ½ cups homemade white sauce

- 1 small egg

- ½ teaspoon salt or to taste

- ½ teaspoon paprika

- ¼ cup milk

- 1 tablespoon fresh parsley, chopped

- 1 can chicken broth

- ½ tablespoon butter

- Hot cooked egg noodles to serve

Method:

1. Add all the ingredients into a bowl except white sauce, butter, broth and noodles.

2. Mix well. Make balls of about 1 ½ inches diameter.

3. Place a skillet over medium heat. Add butter. When butter melts, add meatballs and cook until brown on all the sides.

4. Pour broth and stir. Simmer for 8-10 minutes.

5. Stir in the white sauce. Heat thoroughly.

6. Serve over hot egg noodles.

Pork Chops

Serves: 8

Ingredients:

- 8 pork chops
- Salt to taste
- Pepper to taste
- 2 eggs
- 1 ½ -2 cups breadcrumbs
- Shortening, as required, to fry.

Method:

1. Add salt, pepper and breadcrumbs into a bowl and mix well.

2. Add eggs into another bowl and beat lightly.

3. Dip pork chops in egg. Shake to drop excess egg. Next dredge in breadcrumbs and place on a plate.

4. Place a large skillet over medium heat. Add shortening. When it melts, place pork chops and cook until light brown on both the sides.

5. Remove the pork chops and place in a baking dish. Sprinkle a little water into the skillet. Scrape the bottom of the skillet and pour the water over the pork chops.

6. Bake in a preheated oven at 350 °F for 30-40 minutes or until done.

Fårikål - Norwegian Lamb & Cabbage Stew

Serves: 3-4

Ingredients:

- 2 ¼ pounds lamb meat, cut into large pieces

- 2 ½ tablespoons black peppercorns

- ¾ -1 cup water

- 2 ¼ pounds white cabbage, cut into large wedges

- 1 ½ teaspoons salt

- ¼ cup flour

Method:

1. Add meat into a bowl. Sprinkle flour over it and toss well.

2. Take a soup pot and add water into it. Place a few pieces of lamb at the bottom of the pot. Place a layer of cabbage. Sprinkle a little peppercorn and salt. Repeat these layers with cabbage as the topmost layer.

3. Place the pot over medium heat. Bring to the boil.

4. Lower heat and simmer until meat is cooked. It should take a couple of hours.

5. Serve with steamed potatoes and butter – follow the next recipe.

Smordampete nypoteter - Butter Steamed New Potatoes

Serves: 2

Ingredients:

- ¾ pound new, baby red potatoes

- 3 tablespoons butter + extra to serve

- A handful fresh parsley or dill, chopped

- Salt to taste

- Pepper to taste

Method:

1. Place a skillet over medium heat. Add butter. When butter melts, add potatoes and mix until the potato is well coated. Sprinkle the salt and pepper on it.

2. Lower heat and cover with a lid. Cook the potatoes until they get soft and are well cooked.

3. Transfer into a bowl. Add a blob of butter and stir. Garnish with parsley and serve.

Danish Stegt Flæsk med Persillesovs

Serves: 8

Ingredients:

<u>For stegt flaesk:</u>

- 2.6 pounds pork belly, sliced

- 2 teaspoons salt

- 4 pounds potatoes, scrubbed, cubed

<u>For Persillesovs (parsley sauce):</u>

- 4 tablespoons butter

- 3 cups milk

- 6 tablespoons flour

- 2 bunches parsley, chopped

Method:

4. To make stegt flaesk: Add potatoes into a large pot. Fill with water and 2 teaspoons salt.

5. Bring to the boil. Cook until the potatoes are tender. Drain and set aside.

6. Place pork slices on a baking sheet.

7. Bake in a preheated oven at 350 °F until crisp. Turn the pork slices a couple of times while it is baking.

8. Meanwhile, make the parsley sauce as follows: Place a skillet over medium heat. Add butter. When butter melts, add flour and stir.

9. Add milk stirring constantly. Keep stirring until thick. Add parsley and salt and simmer for a couple of minutes.

10. Serve pork with potatoes and parsley sauce.

Swedish Caviar Cake

Serves: 4

Ingredients:

- 1.5 ounces black caviar like paddlefish roe

- 1.5 ounces red caviar like trout roe

- 1 ½ cups whole milk

- Butter, to grease

- 1/3 cup red onion, finely chopped

- ½ teaspoon salt

- Freshly ground pepper to taste

- 4 large eggs

- 2 teaspoons fresh dill, finely chopped

- ¾ cup crème fraiche

Method:

1. Place a saucepan with milk over medium heat. When it boils, turn off the heat.

2. Add salt and let it cool.

3. Grease a small baking dish with a little butter.

4. Pour 2 -3 cups water into a saucepan and place over low heat. Let it simmer.

5. Whisk together eggs and milk in a bowl.

6. Pour into the baking dish. Cover the dish with foil. Place the dish in a roasting pan. Pour the simmering water into the roasting pan. The water should reach up to at least half the length of the baking dish.

7. Place rack in the center of the oven. Place the roasting pan in a preheated oven.

8. Bake at 325 °F for about 30 minutes or until set and a knife comes out clean when inserted in the center.

9. Uncover and place the baking dish on a cooling rack. When it cools completely, chill for an hour.

10. When the custard cools, spread the crème fraiche over the custard.

11. Place onion, black caviar and red caviar in rows, diagonally. Sprinkle dill and pepper and serve.

Gravadlax in Dill

Serves: 2-3

Ingredients:

- 1.4 pounds salmon fillet, with tail on

- 0.8 ounces salt

- 1.6 ounces sugar

- ½ bunch dill, finely chopped

- 5-6 whole white peppercorns, coarsely crushed

Method:

1. Place the salmon with its skin side down on a rimmed baking sheet.

2. Add dill, pepper, salt and sugar into a bowl. Mix together with your fingers and massage the mixture for a while.

3. Sprinkle this mixture over the salmon. Refrigerate for 2-3 days.

4. Slice into thin slices or use the whole fillet.

5. To use, sear the fillet on a pan and serve.

Kryddad Raudkal Med Blaberjum - Spiced Cabbage with Blueberries

Serves: 3-4

Ingredients:

- 1 tablespoon unsalted butter

- 1 cup fresh blueberries

- 2 tablespoons red wine vinegar

- ½ teaspoon ground ginger

- 1 small Granny Smith apple, cored, peeled, roughly chopped

- 1 small red onion, thinly sliced

- 1 cup red currant jam

- 1 teaspoon ground cinnamon

- 1 medium head red cabbage, cored, thinly sliced

- Kosher salt to taste

- Freshly ground black pepper to taste

Method:

1. Place a large skillet over medium high heat. Add butter. When butter melts, add onions and sauté until translucent.

2. Add rest of the ingredients and 2 tablespoons water and stir. When it begins to boil, lower heat and cover with a lid. Cook until cabbage is tender.

3. Serve hot.

Danish Spinach with Pasta

Serves: 5-6

Ingredients:

- 8 slices bread, discard crust
- 4 cloves garlic, peeled, minced
- 9 ounces cheese, grated
- 2 teaspoons dried oregano
- Salt to taste
- Pepper to taste
- 10.5 ounces whole grain pasta
- 6 tablespoons olive oil
- 2 teaspoons dried basil
- 2 pounds frozen spinach leaves
- 10-12 tomatoes, sliced

Method:

1. Add bread, cheese, garlic, basil and oregano into a bowl.

2. Take a large baking dish and grease with a little butter.

3. Make layers of bread mixture, spinach, pasta and tomatoes. Finally, top with the bread mixture.

4. Drizzle oil over it.

5. Bake in a preheated oven at 350 °F until top is golden brown.

Rødkålssalat Med Appelsin

Serves:

Ingredients:

- 1 medium red cabbage, thinly sliced

- 6 oranges, peeled, separated into segments, chopped

- ¼ cup walnuts

- 1 large swede (rutabaga), grated

- Parsley, to garnish

- Sunflower seed dressing or orange dressing, as required

Method:

1. Add all the ingredients into a bowl and toss well.

2. Garnish with parsley and serve.

Lammekolle pa Gronsager

Serves:

Ingredients:

- 1.3 pounds leg of lamb
- Salt to taste
- Pepper to taste
- 3.3 pounds potatoes, peeled, sliced
- 1 teaspoon dried rosemary
- 2 teaspoons water
- 9 cloves garlic, peeled, minced
- 3.5 ounces ketchup
- 2 teaspoons white wine

Method:

1. Grease a baking dish with a little butter or oil. Add water and white wine and swirl the dish so that it spreads.

2. Place the potato slices on the baking dish.

3. Sprinkle a little of each - salt, pepper, garlic and rosemary.

4. Place lamb over the potatoes.

5. Sprinkle salt, pepper, remaining garlic and rosemary over it.

6. Bake in a preheated oven at 390 °F until meat is tender.

7. Sprinkle more water over the potatoes if required.

8. Slice the meat and serve with potatoes, bread and salad of your choice.

Skinkefars med broccolifyld

Serves: 8

Ingredients:

- 2.2 pounds minced pork

- 3 teaspoons dried basil

- 2 onions, chopped

- 7 ounces breadcrumbs

- 1 large head broccoli, cut into florets

- 3-4 teaspoons salt

- Pepper to taste

- 1 teaspoon nutmeg, grated

- 2 eggs

- Water, as required

For baked potatoes:

- 1 ½ - 2 pounds small potatoes, scrubbed, halved

- Olive oil to drizzle

- Salt to taste

- Herbs of your choice

Method:

1. Add pork, onion, nutmeg, salt, pepper, basil, breadcrumbs and a sprinkle of water into a bowl and mix well. Set aside for 30 minutes.

2. Meanwhile, blanch the broccoli in boiling water for 2 minutes.

3. Drain and set aside.

4. Take a large baking dish. Add half the meat mixture in the dish. Spread it evenly.

5. Sprinkle broccoli all over the meat.

6. Spread the remaining half of meat mixture over the broccoli.

7. Bake in a preheated oven at 390 °F until meat is tender. It should take 40-60 minutes.

8. To make baked potatoes: Add potatoes into a baking dish such that the cut side is facing up.

9. Trickle oil over it. Sprinkle salt and the herbs you are using.

10. Bake in a preheated oven at 390 °F until potatoes are tender. You can place it along with the meatloaf while it is baking.

11. Serve with baked potatoes.

Pan Seared White Fish with Mussels, Cabbage Shoots and Cream

Serves: 2

Ingredients:

For mussels and cabbage:

- 1 cup dry white wine

- ½ cup heavy cream

- ½ tablespoon unsalted butter

- 1 pound mussels, cleaned

- ¼ teaspoon kosher salt + extra

- ½ pound cabbage shoots like kale shoots or baby kale

For fish:

- 2 non-oily fish fillets like pike, trout, perch, etc., boneless, skin-on

- 1 teaspoon unsalted butter

- ½ tablespoon olive oil

Method:

1. To make mussels: Pour white wine into a heavy pot. When it begins to boil, stir in the mussels and cover with a lid.

2. Shake the pot every few minutes until a lot of the mussels open up. It should take about 2 minutes.

3. Remove with a slotted spoon and place in a bowl. Cover and keep warm. Rinse the pot and set aside.

4. Place a fine wire mesh strainer in a cup and pour mussel juice. Pour the mussel juice into a small pot.

5. Place the pot over medium high heat and cook until it is 2/3 its original quantity.

6. Lower heat to medium heat. Stir in the cream and simmer until it slightly reduces in quantity. Add salt and stir. Turn off the heat.

7. To make fish: Place the fish fillets, with the skin side facing up. Make small slits, at every 1-inch on the skin.

8. Flip sides and sprinkle salt on the flesh side. Chill for 2 hours.

9. Place a heavy bottomed skillet over medium heat. Add oil. When the oil is heated, place fish with the skin side facing down. Keep pressing the fish down slightly with a spatula for 5-10 seconds so that it does not curl.

10. When the fish is half cooked, add butter.

11. When butter melts, flip sides of the fish. Turn off the heat. Tilt the pan and spoon the melted butter on the top of the fish.

12. Mildly pat the fish with paper towels if desired to remove excess butter. Keep warm.

13. To make cabbage: Place a pot over high heat. Add ½ cup water, butter and a large pinch salt.

14. When the water begins to boil, stir in the cabbage shoots. Cook until it wilts.

15. Stir in the mussels and heat.

16. Transfer into a strainer that is placed on a bowl. Discard the strained liquid.

17. Add cream into a bowl and fluff lightly with an immersion blender if desired.

18. Pour the cream over mussels and cabbage sprouts. Serve along with fish.

Chapter Four: Norwegian Soup Recipes

Knefla Soup

Serves: 3

Ingredients:

<u>For soup:</u>

- 3 potatoes, peeled, chopped

- 1 medium carrot, peeled, sliced

- 1 onion, chopped

- 1 small stalk celery, sliced

- ½ tablespoon dried parsley

- 2 chicken bouillon cubes

- 2 ½ cups water

- Pepper to taste

- Salt to taste

- 3 tablespoons butter or margarine

For knefla:

- 1 cup all-purpose flour + extra to dust

- ½ teaspoon salt

- 1 small egg

- 6 ounces evaporated milk

- ½ cup milk

Method:

19. Add all the soup ingredients into a soup pot.

1. Place the soup pot over medium heat. Bring to the boil.

2. Lower heat and simmer until vegetables are tender.

3. Meanwhile, add all the knefla ingredients except evaporated milk into a bowl and mix to form dough.

4. Roll the dough on your countertop that is dusted with a little flour until it is thin.

5. Cut into strips lengthwise and cut again into smaller pieces widthwise.

6. Add the strips into the soup pot and continue simmering for 15-20 minutes.

7. Stir in the evaporated milk. Heat thoroughly.

8. Ladle into soup bowls and serve.

Creamy Spinach Soup with Dill

Serves: 6

Ingredients:

- 1 ½ cups curly spinach, discard stems

- 3 tablespoons all-purpose flour

- 6 cups chicken stock or low sodium broth

- 3 tablespoons fresh dill, chopped + extra to garnish

- ¼ teaspoon freshly ground nutmeg

- 3 tablespoons unsalted butter

- 3 small shallots, finely chopped

- 1 ½ cups heavy cream

- Kosher salt to taste

- White pepper powder to taste

- 3 eggs, hard boiled, peeled, quartered, to garnish

Method:

1. Blanch spinach for 2-3 minutes in a pot of boiling water to which salt is added.

2. Drain and plunge into a bowl of chilled water immediately.

3. Drain and squeeze the spinach of excess moisture. Chop the spinach into smaller pieces.

4. Place a large saucepan over medium heat. Add butter. When butter melts, add flour and stir until golden brown.

5. Stir in the shallots and sauté until soft.

6. Add stock and whisk well. Stir constantly and bring to the boil.

7. Let it simmer for 5-6 minutes.

8. Add cream and dill and simmer until slightly thick. Add spinach and turn off the heat.

9. Blend with an immersion blender until smooth. Alternately, blend in a blender until smooth.

10. Add salt, pepper and nutmeg. Stir until well combined.

11. Ladle into soup bowls. Garnish with egg and serve.

Hvidløgssuppe

Serves: 6

Ingredients:

- 22 cloves garlic, peeled, chopped

- 3 leeks, sliced

- 1 ½ bell peppers, diced

- 1 ½ cans (14.5 ounces each) chopped tomatoes

- 1 cup white wine

- Salt, as per taste

- Cayenne Pepper, as per taste

- Pepper powder to taste

- 3 tablespoons olive oil

- 1 bunch parsley, chopped

- 2-3 tablespoons white flour

- 6 cups chicken stock

Method:

1. Place a soup pot over medium heat. Add oil. When the oil is heated, add garlic and sauté for a few seconds until fragrant. Retain a little parsley.

2. Stir in leeks, peppers and rest of the parsley and sauté for a couple of minutes.

3. Sprinkle flour and mix well. Stir in the tomatoes and stock. Bring to the boil.

4. Lower heat and simmer for 20-25 minutes.

5. Add salt, cayenne pepper and pepper.

6. Ladle into soup bowls. Garnish with parsley that was set aside.

7. Serve along with fresh toast.

Scandinavian Cabbage Soup

Serves: 9-10

Ingredients:

- ¾ stick butter
- 1 ½ cups onions, chopped
- 1 ½ cups carrot, thinly sliced
- 4 ½ cups cabbage, chopped
- 1 ½ cups celery, chopped
- 1 ½ cups frozen peas
- 1 ½ cans (14 ½ ounces each) cream style corn
- 3 cups milk
- 1 ½ teaspoons dried thyme
- ½ teaspoon pepper powder
- ½ teaspoon garlic powder
- 3 cups cheddar cheese, shredded
- 1 ½ teaspoons salt
- 3 cups chicken broth

Method:

1. Place a soup pot over medium heat. Add butter. When butter melts, add onions, cabbage, carrots and celery and sauté for a few minutes until tender.

2. Stir in the rest of the ingredients except cheese. Mix well.

3. Lower heat and simmer for 15-20 minutes. Stir in the cheese and keep stirring until cheese melts.

4. Ladle into soup bowls.

5. Serve right away.

Squashsuppe

Serves: 3-4

Ingredients:

- 1.1 pounds squash, peeled, cubed

- ½ tablespoon butter

- 2 cups chicken stock

- ½ teaspoon dried basil

- 1 pasteurized egg yolk

- 1 tablespoon chopped onion

- ½ tablespoon oil

- Pepper, as per taste

- Salt, as per taste

- ¼ cup parmesan cheese, grated

Method:

1. Place a soup pot over medium heat. Add oil and butter. When butter melts, add onions and squash and sauté for a few minutes until onion turns translucent.

2. Stir in the stock. Bring to a boil.

3. Lower heat and simmer until squash is soft.

4. Whisk together yolk and cheese and add into the soup. Turn off the heat the moment you add the yolk mixture. Stir until well combined.

5. Add salt and pepper and stir.

6. Serve with croutons.

Grøn Løgsuppe

Serves: 2-3

Ingredients:

- 1 medium onion, sliced

- 2 large leeks, sliced

- ½ bunch chives

- 2-3 potatoes, peeled, cubed

- 2 tablespoons butter

- 2 cups stock

- ½ package cream cheese

- Salt, as per taste

- Pepper, as per taste

- ¼ cup heavy cream

- A handful fresh basil, chopped to garnish

Method:

1. Place a soup pot over medium heat. Add butter. When butter melts, add onions and leek and sauté for a couple of minutes.

2. Add potatoes and stir well.

3. Lower heat and cook for 10 minutes.

4. Stir in stock, salt, pepper and chives. Cook until the potatoes are tender. Turn off the heat.

5. Transfer into a blender and blend until smooth. Pour it back into the pot.

6. Add about a tablespoon of cream cheese into the pot and stir. Taste and adjust the seasoning if necessary. Reheat the soup.

7. Add remaining cream cheese into a bowl. Add heavy cream. Whip until creamy.

8. Ladle soup into soup bowls. Add a dollop of whipped cream-cream cheese mixture.

9. Sprinkle basil on top. Serve right away with potato bread slices.

Juliennesuppe

Serves: 3-4

- 1 medium onion, sliced

- 1 large leek, julienned

- ½ cup fresh or frozen green peas, thaw if frozen

- 2 potatoes, peeled, julienned

- 1 rutabaga, peeled, julienned

- 2 medium carrots, peeled, julienned

- 1 stick celery, julienned

- 2 tablespoons butter

- 3 cups stock

- Salt, as per taste

- Pepper, as per taste

- A handful fresh parsley, chopped to garnish

Method:

1. Place a soup pot over medium heat. Add butter. When butter melts, add onions and leek and sauté for a couple of minutes.

2. Add potatoes and stir well. Add carrots, rutabaga and celery.

3. Lower heat and cook for 10 minutes.

4. Stir in stock, salt, pepper and green peas. Cook until the vegetables are tender. Turn off the heat.

5. Ladle soup into soup bowls.

6. Sprinkle parsley on top. Serve right away with French bread slices.

Scandinavian Vegetable Soup with Shrimp

Serves: 4

Ingredients:

- 2 carrots, peeled, thinly sliced

- 2 cups cauliflower florets, ½ inch each

- ½ pound green beans, trimmed, cut into ½ inch pieces

- 2 small boiling potatoes, peeled, cut into ¼ inch cubes, soaked in a bowl of water

- 2/3 cup fresh or frozen green peas, thaw if frozen

- 4 ounces fresh spinach, discard hard stems, finely chopped

- 2 large egg yolks

- 2 teaspoons salt

- 4 cups water

- 1 cup half and half

- 2 teaspoons dry sherry (optional)

- ½ pound shrimp, peeled, deveined

- A handful fresh dill, finely chopped

- 4 dill sprigs, to garnish

Method:

1. Drain the potatoes and add into a soup pot. Add cauliflower, carrot, peas, green beans and water into the soup pot.

2. Place the soup pot over medium heat. Cook until vegetables are soft.

3. Add spinach and stir. Cook until spinach wilts.

4. Meanwhile, add yolk and half and half into a bowl and whisk well. Add a little of the cooked vegetable liquid and whisk. Repeat this until about a cup of the cooked liquid is added.

5. Pour into the soup pot. Cook for a minute. Stir constantly.

6. Add shrimp and cook for a minute.

7. Season with salt and pepper. Add sherry and chopped dill and stir. Turn off the heat.

8. Ladle into soup bowls. Garnish with a sprig of dill and serve.

Scandinavian Chicken Soup

Serves: 4

Ingredients:

- 3 pounds whole chicken

- ¾ pound potatoes, peeled, cubed

- 4 cups chicken broth (use the same liquid in which chicken is cooked)

- ¾ cup onion, chopped

- Salt, as per taste

- Pepper, as per taste

- 1 small red onion, chopped

- 1 teaspoon fresh dill, chopped, divided

Method:

1. Add chicken into a soup pot. Pour about 5 cups water. Place the pot over medium heat. Cook until chicken is tender.

2. Strain the water and use 4 cups of the cooked liquid as broth. Add it back into the pot.

3. Place chicken on your cutting board. When cool enough to handle, chop into pieces and discard the bones and skin.

4. Add potatoes, chopped onion and ½ teaspoon dill into the pot. Place the pot over medium heat. Bring to the boil.

5. Lower heat and simmer until soft.

6. Add chicken, salt and pepper and let it cook for 5 minutes. Turn off the heat.

7. Add remaining onions and dill and stir.

8. Ladle into soup bowls and serve.

Kjotsupa - Lamb Soup

Serves: 3-4

Ingredients:

- 1 tablespoon olive oil

- 1 ½ pounds lamb, bone-in

- 3 tablespoons brown rice or rolled oats for a traditional soup

- ¼ teaspoon dried oregano

- ¼ teaspoon dried thyme

- ¼ cabbages, chopped

- ¼ rutabaga, sliced

- 2 potatoes, scrubbed, cut into ½ inch cubes

- ½ cup cauliflower florets

- 1 small onion, sliced

- ½ teaspoon garlic, chopped

- 3 cups water

- 2 carrots, cut into ½ inch pieces

Method:

1. Place a soup pot over medium heat. Add oil. When the oil is heated, add garlic and sauté for about a minute until fragrant.

2. Add lamb and cook until brown. Stir in the onions and sauté until translucent.

3. Add brown rice and water. Increase the heat to high heat. When it begins to boil, discard the scum that is formed on the top. Let it boil for 5 minutes.

4. Lower heat and add herbs. Cover and cook until tender.

5. Add vegetables and cover again. Cook until tender.

6. Remove lamb from the pot with a slotted spoon and place on your cutting board. When cool enough to handle, chop coarsely.

7. Add the lamb back into the pot and let it simmer for 5 minutes.

8. Ladle into soup bowls and serve.

Scandinavian Raspberry Soup

Serves:

Ingredients:

- 3 packages raspberries, frozen in syrup, thawed

- 6 tablespoons lemon juice

- ¾ cup orange juice

- 1 ¼ cups Chablis or any other white wine of your choice

- 1 ½ tablespoons cornstarch

- 2 oranges, peeled, deseeded, separated into segments

For garnishing:

- Orange rinds

- ¼ cup sour cream

- A handful fresh mint leaves

Method:

1. Add 1-½ package raspberries into a blender and blend until smooth.

2. Pass the mixture through a fine wire mesh strainer that is placed over a saucepan.

3. Add oranges juice, cornstarch and lemon juice and stir.

4. Place the saucepan over medium heat. Stir constantly until it thickens slightly and looks clearer. Turn off the heat.

5. Add remaining raspberries and white wine and stir. Cover and refrigerate for 4-5 hours.

6. Divide the orange segments into soup bowls.

7. Ladle soup into bowls. Top with dollops of sour cream and serve.

Kold Sommersuppe

Serves: 8-10

Ingredients:

- 2 cucumbers, chopped

- 2 onions, chopped

- 6 tomatoes, chopped

- 2 green bell pepper, chopped

- 4 cups water

- 28 ounces breadcrumbs

- 2 cloves garlic, peeled, crushed

- 2 tablespoons olive oil

- 4 tablespoons red wine vinegar

- Salt, as per taste

Method:

1. Set aside a little onion, cucumber and green bell pepper and ad rest of it into a blender. Also add breadcrumbs and water. Blend until well combined.

2. Add vinegar, oil, salt and pepper and blend until well combined.

3. Transfer into a bowl. Refrigerate for 6-8 hours.

4. Ladle into soup bowls. Sprinkle the vegetables that were kept aside.

5. Serve with French bread sticks.

Chapter Five: Norwegian Salad Recipes

Celery and Blue Cheese Salad

Serves: 3-4

Ingredients:

- 4-5 celery ribs, chopped into ½ inch thick pieces

- Sea salt to taste

- ½ tablespoon extra-virgin olive oil

- 1.5 ounces blue cheese, crumbled

- Coarsely ground pepper to taste

Method:

1. Add all the ingredients into a bowl and toss well.

2. Chill and serve.

Danish Potato Salad

Serves: 4

Ingredients:

- 2-3 cups potatoes, cooked, cubed

- 2 tablespoons sweet pickle relish

- 1 small onion, chopped

- 2 tablespoons water

- 2 tablespoons vinegar

- 3 tablespoons sugar

- Salt to taste

- Pepper to taste

- 2 eggs, hard boiled

- 1 egg, beaten

- ½ teaspoon mustard

- A handful chopped celery

- ½ cup salad dressing or mayonnaise or any other dressing of your choice

Method:

1. Add sugar, vinegar, water, salt, pepper and mustard into a small saucepan.

2. Place the saucepan over medium heat and bring to the boil.

3. Stir in the beaten egg and stir continuously until the mixture becomes slightly thick. Turn off the heat.

4. Stir in the salad dressing.

5. Add rest of the ingredients into a bowl and toss. Pour the dressing on top. Fold gently.

6. Chill for a few hours and serve.

Danish Cucumber Salad

Serves: 2-3

Ingredients:

- 1 pound English cucumber, cut along the length, deseeded, cut into half inch thick slices

- 1 tablespoon fresh lemon juice

- A handful fresh cilantro or chervil, finely chopped

- 1 tablespoon kosher salt

- 1 tablespoon fresh dill, finely chopped

- Edible flowers of vegetables of your choice, to garnish

Method:

1. Add cucumber, salt and lemon juice into a bowl and toss well. Let it sit for 15-20 minutes.

2. Drain the liquid in the bowl.

3. Add rest of the ingredients and toss well.

4. Top with edible flowers and serve.

Scandinavian Cucumber Salad

Serves: 6-8

Ingredients:

- 1 cup sour cream

- 6 small cucumbers, thinly sliced, do not peel

- 4 tablespoons parsley flakes

- 2 tablespoons sugar

- 5 tablespoons tarragon vinegar

- ¼ cup chives, chopped

Method:

1. Set aside the cucumbers and add rest of the ingredients into a bowl. Stir until well combined and sugar is dissolved.

2. Add cucumber slices and fold gently.

3. Cover and refrigerate for 2-4 hours.

Smoked Salmon Salad

Serves: 3-4

<u>For vinaigrette:</u>

- 1 small shallot, chopped

- 3 tablespoons fresh dill, chopped

- Fine sea Salt, as per taste

- 3 tablespoons extra - virgin olive oil

- 1 very small clove garlic, chopped

- 1/3 cup low fat plain yogurt

- Juice of ½ lemon

<u>For salad:</u>

- 4 cups mixed greens

- 2 eggs, hardboiled, peeled, sliced into rounds

- ½ bunch red radish, thinly sliced into rounds or half-moons depending on the size

- 3 slices Scandinavian crisp bread slices, crumbled

- ½ small fennel bulb, trimmed, halved, thinly sliced

- 2 -3 ounces smoked salmon

- Pepper powder to taste

- ¼ cup fresh dill, chopped

Method:

1. To make vinaigrette: Add shallot, lemon juice, dill, salt, garlic, 2 tablespoons water and yogurt into a blender and blend until smooth.

2. With the blender running, pour oil in a thin drizzle through the feeder tube. Let it blend until the dressing becomes slightly thick.

3. Pour into a bowl. Add more salt if desired. Cover and refrigerate until use.

4. To make salad: Place greens and dill on a serving platter. Mix them up.

5. Place egg slices, fennel slices and radish slices over it.

6. Roll the salmon slices and place over it. Place dressing on the side and serve topped with crisp bread.

Blue Cheese, Grape and Gem Lettuce Salad

Serves: 4

Ingredients:

<u>For dressing:</u>

- 3 tablespoons apple cider vinegar

- 3 tablespoons walnut oil

- 3 tablespoons olive oil

- ½ teaspoon Dijon mustard

- 1 tablespoon crème fraiche

- Freshly ground Pepper, as per taste

- Salt, as per taste

<u>For salad:</u>

- ½ cup walnuts, chopped, toasted

- ½ head celery, use only the inner stems and leaves, thinly slice only the stems

- Flaky sea Salt, as per taste

- ½ pound baby gem lettuce or Bibb lettuce, torn into big pieces

- ¾ cup green grapes, halved

- 1.5 ounces Danish Kornblomst or Stilton blue cheese, crumbled

Method:

1. To make dressing: Add all the dressing ingredients into a bowl and whisk well.

2. Cover and set aside for a while for the flavors to set in.

3. Place lettuce leaves on a serving platter. Place celery stems and leaves over it.

4. Place grapes all over it. Sprinkle walnuts on top. Pour vinaigrette all over the salad. Sprinkle some salt and pepper. Sprinkle blue cheese just before you serve.

Chapter Six: Norwegian Dessert Recipes

Swedish Apple Pie

Makes: 2 pies

Ingredients:

For pie:

- 7 cups peeled, sliced apples
- 1 ½ cups granulated sugar
- 2 eggs
- 1 cup sour cream
- 4 tablespoons flour
- 1/8 teaspoon salt
- 2 teaspoons vanilla extract
- 2 unbaked pie shells (10 inches each)

For topping:

- 2/3 cup sugar
- 2 teaspoons ground cinnamon
- 2/3 cup flour
- 1 cup butter, softened

Method:

1. Add saucepans into a saucepan. Cover with water and place over medium heat. Cook until soft.

2. Drain and add apples into a bowl. Add flour, sugar and salt.

3. Whisk together eggs and vanilla and pour into the bowl of apples.

4. Add sour cream and stir.

5. Spoon the apple mixture into the pie shells.

6. Bake in a preheated oven at 350 °F for about 30-40 minutes or until set.

7. Meanwhile, add flour, sugar, butter and cinnamon into a bowl. Mix until crumbly.

8. When the apple mixture is set, sprinkle the crumbly mixture on top.

9. Bake for 10-15 minutes.

10. Cool for a while. Slice into wedges and serve.

Norwegian Rhubarb Pudding

Serves: 3

Ingredients:

- 14 tablespoons water

- ¾ pound fresh rhubarb, cut into ½ inch pieces

- 1 ½ tablespoons cornstarch mixed with 2 tablespoons water

- ½ cup chilled whipping cream

- 6 tablespoons granulated sugar

- ¼ teaspoon vanilla extract

- 1 tablespoon granulated sugar

Method:

1. Add 14 tablespoons water and 6 tablespoons sugar into a bowl. Place over medium heat.

2. Stir occasionally.

3. When it begins to boil, stir in rhubarb. Simmer until tender.

4. Stir in the cornstarch mixture. Stir constantly until thick.

5. Add vanilla extract and stir.

6. Spoon into dessert bowls. Cover and chill.

7. Meanwhile, add whipping cream and sugar into a chilled bowl. Whip until stiff.

8. Spoon into a piping bag. Pipe on to the pudding

Traditional Swedish Almond Cake

Serves: 20

Ingredients:

- 2 ½ cups sugar

- 3 teaspoons almond extract

- 2 ½ cups flour

- ¼ teaspoon ground cinnamon

- 2 eggs

- 1 1/3 cups milk

- 1 teaspoon baking powder

- 1 cup butter, melted

- Icing sugar to sprinkle

Method:

1. Add sugar, almond extract, eggs and milk into a bowl. Whisk well.

2. Add flour and baking powder and whisk until well combined.

3. Add cinnamon and whisk again. Add butter and stir.

4. Grease a baking dish and pour the batter in it.

5. Bake in a preheated oven at 350 °F for about 50 minutes or until a knife enter comes out clean with inserted in the center of the cake

6. Let the cake cool on a wired rack.

7. Sprinkle icing sugar on top. Slice and serve.

Norwegian Cookies

Makes: 70-80 cookies

Ingredients:

- 2 cups butter

- 2 eggs, beaten

- 2 teaspoons almond extract

- 2 cups sugar

- 4 cups flour

- 45-50 maraschino cherries, halved

Method:

1. Add butter and sugar into a bowl and beat until creamy.

2. Add eggs and beat until well combined.

3. Add flour and almond extract and mix into dough.

4. Chill for a couple of hours.

5. Make small balls of the dough. Press on cookie sheets lined with parchment paper and press the dough lightly.

6. Press a cherry half on each cookie.

7. Bake in a preheated oven at 350 °F for about 15 minutes or until light brown on the edges.

8. Let it cool for 5-8 minutes. Remove the cookies with a metal spatula. Cool on a wire rack completely.

9. Sprinkle powdered sugar on top and serve.

Swedish Brownies

Makes: 25-30 pieces

Ingredients:

- 3 eggs

- 1 ½ cups granulated sugar

- 1 ½ teaspoons almond flavoring or lemon flavoring or anise flavoring

- 1 ½ cups all-purpose flour

- ¾ cup butter or margarine, melted

- A handful nuts, chopped (optional)

Method:

1. Add eggs into a bowl. Beat until light.

2. Add sugar and whisk well. Stir in the flour. Mix until well combined

3. Add the flavoring that you are using.

4. Pour into a square baking dish that is greased with a little oil or butter.

5. Sprinkle nuts on top if using.

6. Bake in a preheated oven at 350 °F for about 30-40 minutes or until a knife comes out clean when inserted in the center.

7. Let the brownies cool on a wired rack. Chop into squares and serve.

Tilsorte Bondepiker - Veiled Peasant Girls

Serves: 4-6

Ingredients:

- 1 pound apples, peeled, cored, quartered

- ½ ounce butter

- Sugar to taste

- 2- 2 ½ ounces breadcrumbs, oven dried

- Whipped cream to top

Method:

1. Add sugar and apples into a saucepan.

2. Place the saucepan over low heat. Cook until soft. Mash the apples.

3. Place a frying pan over medium heat. Add butter. When butter melts, add breadcrumbs and sugar and sauté until golden brown. Be careful, as the breadcrumbs tend to burn.

4. Turn off the heat and cool.

5. Take a bowl and make alternate layers of breadcrumbs and apple. Top with whipped cream and serve.

6. The other option is to make alternate layers of breadcrumbs and apple in a small baking dish.

7. Sprinkle sugar on top. Place small pieces of butter at different spots.

8. Bake in a preheated oven at 350 °F for about 30 minutes.

9. Cool for a while. Top with whipped cream and serve.

Ostkak - Swedish Cheesecake

Serves: 2-4

Ingredients:

- 0.9 pound cottage cheese, strained

- 2 tablespoons granulated sugar

- ¼ cup almond meal

- 2 large eggs

- 2 tablespoons all-purpose flour

- 2-3 apricot kernels or bitter almonds, ground

Method:

1. Add eggs into a bowl. Whisk until fluffy.

2. Add sugar, cottage cheese and flour and mix well.

3. Add apricot kernels and mix well.

4. Pour into a baking dish that is greased with a little butter.

5. Bake in a preheated oven at 225 °F for about 30-45 minutes. When it begins to brown, cover the dish with foil and bake.

6. Cool for a while and serve lukewarm.

Norwegian Apple Cake

Serves: 12-15

Ingredients:

- 1 ½ cups butter, softened

- 3 cups self-raising flour

- 8 apples, peeled, cored, sliced

- 2 cups + 2 tablespoons sugar

- 4 eggs, beaten

- 2 teaspoons ground cinnamon

Method:

1. Add butter and sugar into a bowl. Beat with an electric mixer until light, creamy and pale yellow in color.

2. Add eggs and beat well.

3. Add flour, a little at a time and beat well each time.

4. Pour the mixture into a square baking dish.

5. Place the apple slices on the batter, close to each other.

6. Mix together sugar and cinnamon in a bowl. Sprinkle over the apple layer.

7. Bake in a preheated oven at 350 °F for about 60 minutes or until golden brown in color.

8. Cool and serve either warm or cold. Top with crème fraiche if desired and serve.

Bringebaerpudding med Bringebaersaus - Raspberry Pudding with Raspberries Sauce

Serves: 8

Ingredients:

<u>For raspberry pudding:</u>

- 17.5 ounces raspberries

- 3 tablespoons sugar

- 30 ounces vanilla quark or vanilla yogurt

- 4 tablespoons water

- 8 gelatin sheets

- Seeds from 1 pod vanilla

<u>For sauce:</u>

- 9 ounces raspberries

- Juice of 2 lemons

- 3.5 ounces icing sugar

<u>For topping:</u>

- 8 raspberries

- Mint leaves

Method:

1. To make pudding: Add gelatin sheets into a bowl of cold water. Let it soak for 5-6 minutes.

2. Add 14 ounces raspberries, water, sugar and vanilla seeds into a saucepan.

3. Place the saucepan over medium heat. Bring to the boil. Stir constantly until sugar dissolves. Turn off the heat.

4. Drain the water from the gelatin sheets and squeeze as much water as possible. Place the gelatin sheets in raspberry syrup. Let it cool completely.

5. Add vanilla quark and remaining raspberries and stir gently.

6. Spoon the mixture into 8 dessert glasses. Chill for 2-4 hours.

7. To make raspberry sauce: Add all the sauce ingredients into a small saucepan. Place the saucepan over medium heat. Cook until raspberries are slightly soft.

8. Turn off the heat and cool.

9. Pour sauce over the pudding. Garnish with a raspberry on each glass. Place mint leaves on top and serve

Strawberry Snow

Serves: 4

Ingredients:

- ½ pound strawberries, hulled

- ¼ cup caster sugar

- ¼ teaspoon vanilla extract

- Mint leaves to garnish

- 1 large egg white, at room temperature

- ¼ cup whipping cream

- 3-4 strawberries, sliced, to garnish

Method:

1. Add strawberries into a blender and blend until smooth.

2. Transfer into a bowl. Add egg white and sugar and beat until it turns stiff and shiny.

3. Add vanilla and cream into another bowl and whip until peaks are formed.

4. Transfer cream into the bowl of strawberries. Fold gently.

5. Divide into 4 dessert bowls. Top with strawberry slices and mint leaves. Cover with cling wrap.

6. Chill for a while and serve.

Norwegian Fruit Cake

Makes: 20-25 slices

Ingredients:

- 17.6 ounces butter, at room temperature

- 10 eggs

- 2 teaspoons baking powder

- 8.8 ounces currants

- Pearl sugar, as required

- 17.6 ounces sugar

- 17.6 ounces flour

- Juice of 2 large lemons

- Zest of 2 large lemons

- Ground or flaked almonds, as required

Method:

1. Add butter and sugar into a bowl. Beat with blender until it turns fluffy and creamy.

2. Add each egg one after the other and beat well each time.

3. Whisk well for a few seconds until light.

4. Add lemon zest and juice and stir.

5. Mix together flour and baking powder and add into the batter. Mix until smooth.

6. Add currants and fold gently.

7. Pour into a greased baking dish. Sprinkle pearl sugar and flaked almond on top.

8. Bake in a preheated oven at 350 °F for about 30-40 minutes or until a knife comes out clean when inserted in the center

9. Let the cake cool on a wired rack.

10. Slice and serve.

Almond Sugar Cookies

Makes: 4 ½ dozens

Ingredients:

- 4 ½ sticks unsalted butter, softened

- 6 cups all-purpose flour+ extra for dusting

- 2 small eggs, beaten with 1-2 tablespoons water

- 1 cup + 1/3 cup sugar

- 1 ½ teaspoons kosher salt

- ¾ cup almonds, finely chopped

Method:

1. Add flour, salt and baking powder into a bowl. Mix well.

2. Add butter and 1-cup sugar into a mixing bowl. Beat with an electric mixer at medium high speed until it turns fluffy and pale in color.

3. Lower the speed to low speed. Add the dry mixture and mix it well until it is well combined. Do not overbeat.

4. Dust your countertop with a little flour. Roll out the dough into a rectangle of about ½ inch thickness.

5. Brush egg mixture all over it. Sprinkle almonds and remaining sugar over it.

6. Chop into squares or rectangles.

7. Place on baking trays. Leave a gap of about an inch between cookies.

8. Place rack in the center of the oven.

9. Bake in a preheated oven at 350°F for about 15 minutes or until the sides are beginning to turn golden brown.

10. Remove from the oven and cool for 3-4 minutes. Remove the cookies carefully with a metal spatula and cool on a wire rack. Store in an airtight container.

Ostkaka med Farska Jordgubbar Och Mynta – Almond Cheesecake with Macerated Strawberries and Mint

Serves: 6

Ingredients:

- 9 tablespoons sugar

- 1/3 cup mint, minced

- 4 ½ cups strawberries, quartered

- 9 tablespoons milk

- 9 tablespoons almonds, blanched

- 9 tablespoons heavy cream

- 2 eggs

- Whipped cream to serve

- Unsalted butter, to grease

- 1 ¾ cups cottage cheese, drained for 7-8 hours

- 3 tablespoons flour

- Confectioner's sugar, to garnish

Method:

1. Add ½ cup sugar, strawberries and mint into a bowl. Mix well and stir. Set aside for an hour.

2. Add remaining sugar and almonds into the food processor bowl and pulse until finely ground.

3. Add heavy cream, cottage cheese, flour, milk and eggs and pulse until smooth. Pour into a greased, round or oval baking dish.

4. Bake in a preheated oven at 350 °F for 30-45 minutes or until brown and slightly puffy.

5. When done, cool for a while. Sprinkle confectioner's sugar. Serve with the strawberry and mint mixture topped with whipped cream.

Drommekage – Danish Dream Cake

Serves: 5-6

Ingredients:

- 7 ½ tablespoons unsalted butter, softened + extra to grease

- 1 cup whole milk

- 3 small eggs

- 1 teaspoon vanilla extract

- ½ cup packed dark brown sugar

- 1 ¾ + 2 tablespoons all-purpose flour + extra to dust the pan

- ¾ cup + 2 tablespoons sugar

- ½ tablespoon baking powder

- ¾ cup shredded coconut, sweetened

Method:

1. Grease a small spring form pan of about 6 inches with a little butter. Dust with a little flour.

2. Set aside 2 tablespoons of milk and add rest of the milk into a saucepan. Add 3 tablespoons butter. Place the saucepan over medium heat.

3. When butter melts, turn off the heat and set aside to cool.

4. Add sugar and eggs into a bowl. Whisk well using a hand mixer until it turns pale yellow and frothy.

5. Add flour and baking powder and whisk until well combined.

6. Add vanilla and whisk again. Add milk and fold gently.

7. Pour the batter in the prepared baking pan. Line a baking sheet with parchment paper. Place the baking pan over it.

8. Bake in a preheated oven at 350 °F for about 50 minutes or until a toothpick when inserted in the center comes out clean.

9. Remove from the oven and cool.

10. Raise the temperature of the oven to 400 °F.

11. Add remaining butter, remaining milk, brown sugar and coconut into a saucepan. Place the saucepan over medium heat.

12. Heat until brown sugar dissolves completely. Stir constantly. Turn off the heat.

13. Spoon the mixture over the baked cake. Place it back in the oven and bake until the mixture begins to bubble and the coconut becomes lightly toasted.

14. Cool completely on a wire rack. Remove from the spring form pan and place on a plate.

15. Slice and serve.

Kladdkaka – Swedish "Gooey" Chocolate Cake

Serves: 12

Ingredients:

- 15 tablespoons unsalted butter, melted, cooled + extra to grease

- 1 ½ cups sugar

- 3 teaspoons vanilla extract

- 3 large eggs

- Whipped cream to serve

- 1/3 cup plain bread crumbs

- 10 ½ tablespoons natural cocoa powder

- ¼ teaspoon + a pinch salt

- 1 ½ cups cake flour, sifted

Method:

1. Grease a small spring form pan of about 12 inches with a little butter. Sprinkle breadcrumbs over the buttered area. Shake off the excess breadcrumbs and discard it.

2. Add butter, sugar, cocoa powder, salt and vanilla into a bowl and whisk well.

3. Add an egg at a time and beat well each time. Add flour and fold gently.

4. Spoon the batter into the prepared baking pan.

5. Bake in a preheated oven at 400 °F for about 10 minutes and until jiggling in the center. A thin film will have formed on the top but the center will be gooey.

6. Remove from the oven and cool.

7. Place in the refrigerator for a couple of hours.

8. Remove the cake from the mold and serve.

Honey and Butter Baked Pears with Cold Cream

Serves: 4

Ingredients:

- 4 Anjou pears, peeled, halved, cored

- Kosher Salt, as per taste

- 1 fresh bay leaf, chopped

- Chilled crème fraiche or heavy cream to serve

- 4 tablespoons unsalted butter, cut into small cubes of about ½ inch

- 3 sprigs thyme

- ¼ cup honey

Method:

1. Place a sheet of parchment paper on a rimmed baking sheet. Place the pears on it with the cut side facing up. Do not overlap.

2. Place butter cubes over the pear halves. Sprinkle salt, bay leaf and thyme over the pear halves.

3. Drizzle honey over it.

4. Bake in a preheated oven at 400 °F until tender. Baste in the melted butter and honey (from the rimmed baking sheet) every 15 minutes until golden brown. It should take about an hour.

5. When done, serve hot with chilled cream on top.

Conclusion

Thank you once again for choosing this book!

I hope you found the recipes mentioned in this book easy to cook. There is no question about the taste and the authenticity of these recipes. To give a complete Norwegian experience, we have segregated the recipes under breakfast, lunch, dinner and desserts.

The ingredients used in all these recipes are easily available and the recipes are fairly simple to follow. Even if you are a novice cook, you will be able to prepare these lip-smacking Norwegian recipes like a pro, provided you follow the directions for these recipes to the T.

I hope you have fun trying these recipes. I want to thank you once again for choosing this book.

Bon Appetit!

Other Books by Grizzly Publishing

"Jamaican Cookbook: Traditional Jamaican Recipes Made Easy"

https://www.amazon.com/dp/B07B68KL8D

"Brazilian Instant Pot Cookbook: Delicious Pressure Cooked Meals Made Fast and Easy"

https://www.amazon.com/dp/B078XBYP89

"Norwegian Cookbook: Traditional Scandinavian Recipes Made Easy"

https://www.amazon.com/dp/B079M2W223

"Casserole Cookbook: Delicious Casserole Recipes From Around The World"

https://www.amazon.com/dp/B07B6GV61Q

CPSIA information can be obtained
at www.ICGtesting.com
Printed in the USA
LVHW020020160222
711186LV00003B/204